THE LAST GREAT BATTLE OF THE INDIAN WARS

Henry M. Jackson, Forrest J. Gerard
and the campaign for the self-determination
of America's Indian tribes

MARK N. TRAHANT

For information about discounts for bulk sales,
please contact The Cedars Group,
208-968-4642 or at sales@thecedarsgroup.org

Indexed by Samantha Miller / Sciendex
Book design by JiaYing Grygiel

ISBN: 978-0-9827581-0-6

TABLE OF CONTENTS

A Good Time For Indians, Really

P. Sam Deloria

Sometimes conventional wisdom is pretty accurate; sometimes, often, it oversimplifies; sometimes it is just wrong. Conventional wisdom holds that the late Sen. Henry Jackson of the state of Washington, formerly a stalwart of the dreaded federal policy of termination (of the federal-tribal relationship between the United States and Indian tribes as political entities), cynically changed his stripes to become an architect of the new mirror-image federal policy of tribal self-determination, which was to reach its full flower in the 1970s, his motivation being to clean up his race relations credentials for a run for the presidency beginning in 1972 and perhaps beyond.

Jackson's turnaround escaped criticism at the time because federal Indian policy is not one of the benchmarks scrutinized by press and public during a presidential campaign, and it was certainly not in the interests of Indian and Native leadership to call him into question on this point. Given the epochal Indian self-determination policy articulated by the Nixon administration in 1970 and thereafter, there was certainly little chance that, had Jackson ever posed a serious threat as a candidate, the opposing party would have seen an advantage in criticizing him for embracing a policy they could reasonably see as theirs.

It was a good time for Indians, really. Fresh from the very real threat of termination, suddenly the Indian tribes found themselves the subject of a competition among presidential candidates as to who could do more for them. And that contest was intensified by the precursor of the 1972 shocker "Nixon Goes To China." Richard M. Nixon, the vice president of the United States during the administration most identified with the termination policy (with arguable fairness, given the role of various Democrats in conceiving and perpetuating termination), was outdoing the Democrats as the Indians' friend.

In this book, veteran journalist Mark Trahant, a member of the Shoshone-Bannock Tribes of the Fort Hall Reservation in Idaho, examines the basis for the conventional wisdom and looks at Jackson's undeniable turnaround in some detail, revealing it to be one of the most remarkable reversals in American political history. The history of federal Indian policy is not a major focus of American historians, but it is worthy of note that not many instances exist of a major political figure reversing his field so utterly on a matter of policy with which he had come to be strongly identified, although this identification was not really part of Jackson's national image. His national reputation rested largely on defense and foreign policy. Jackson's change does not rank with Lyndon Johnson's breathtaking and historically more far-reaching embrace of civil rights as president, but it is noteworthy in itself. Johnson's civil rights policies and views had been cannily obscured in the public mind for years prior to his presidency, to position him for an eventual presidential run of his own, so Jackson's reversal was more dramatic and noticeable.

Regardless of Jackson's sincerity, his fateful choice of a staff aide to carry out his new policy committed him irrevocably to making positive history from the Indians' point of view. Forrest Gerard, a Blackfeet who had wide experience in tribal affairs with both the legislative and executive branches of the federal government, was hired as a staff assistant on the Senate Interior Committee, the committee then having jurisdiction over Indian affairs. Gerard was far too savvy to undertake the position if it looked like window-dressing, and his knowledge of the issues and his intuition enabled him to orchestrate the development and passage of major legislation, the most remarkable outpouring of positive legislation in the history of federal-tribal affairs. This legislative period continued after the end of the Jackson-Gerard combination for several years until and after Gerard left the committee to become the first assistant secretary of interior for Indian affairs in the nation's history, during the Carter administration. From that position, he was able to implement much of the legislation he had helped create and shepherd through the Congress. It was a remarkable opportunity to reshape this fundamental federal-tribal relationship, and a virtually unprecedented opportunity to be a one-man band, writing legislation and then scurrying down Pennsylvania Avenue to put it into effect. Gerard made the most of it.

The cliché holds that journalism is the first draft of history, and Trahant is a journalist and not a historian. This book, then, by telling the who, what, when, where and how, lays the groundwork for a host of historical studies of this period and perhaps of this unusual team of senator and aide. Although much has changed in America and American politics in the intervening years, we don't know until we look more deeply into the workings of the period what lessons are there to be learned from this case.

In the meantime, Trahant has provided a considerable service by calling our attention to the facts about Jackson and Gerard and by giving us an account of a short but rich period during which major steps were taken to give a positive foundation to the federal-tribal relationship and the concept of Indian self-determination – a period whose effect is still being felt daily by Indian people and all residents of Indian reservations throughout the country.

One question this book does not answer, probably because Trahant lacked access to people with intimate knowledge of Jackson's thinking (if there ever were such people) who might have hazarded an answer: Did Jackson "convert" to a set of policies that would ensure major strengthening of the powers of tribal governments for more than a generation, or was his conversion strictly tactical and cynical? In my view, this kind of question is little more than gossip, although it is of interest to those with boundless appetite for insight into political motivations. But I have always thought that Native people spend too much effort worrying about whether a particular state or national politician likes, really genuinely likes Indians – and too often are fooled by the answers they think they get. Rather, in my own view of politics, it doesn't matter what a politician thinks as much as what he or she does. In this case, I don't think the answer matters much, and it is good that Trahant doesn't spend a lot of speculation on it.

Several themes emerge in the course of this work that in the future should be explicitly explored and elucidated by Trahant and others with his insight and energy. One is the importance of termination as the lodestar of federal Indian policy for the government and the Indians alike. For more than 60 years, tribes have tended to measure all policy and policy proposals according to a termination template, and those on the federal side have at least implicitly allowed the fear and the threat of termination to keep the "Indian" federal Indian policy within bounds. This "boogeyman" approach has pre-empted more substantive discussions of federal Indian policy for a very long time, continues to underlie much of the debate and stagnates policy development.

A second theme involves the hidden layers of personality, loyalty and obligation that influence politics and policy. Analysts, scholars and historians frequently occupy themselves with abstractions concerning tribal sovereignty, congressional plenary power and such matters, when the origin and perpetuation of objectionable policies may be more related to a particular senator's position dictated by local politics and the ripple effect of other senators steering clear of that position out of loyalty, obligation or respect. Sometimes the preoccupation with Indians As The Center Of History overlooks the simple fact that Clinton Anderson was Jackson's mentor and Anderson had reasons to view tribal interests differently from many of his colleagues.

A related set of issues involves whether and how opportunities can be squandered. It was merely luck that Gerard was the right person to make the most of Jackson's "conversion." A different, less canny and experienced person may have let Jackson off the hook and produced nothing but cosmetic measures designed to placate the tribes but not change the system. It is not clear that present national tribal leadership is able to respond appropriately to such opportunities and to keep the right kind of pressure on a party or an administration. We must concede that the historical record is replete with examples of assistant secretaries unable to hold their administrations to a high standard of follow-through.

And finally, one hopes, probably in vain, that the cargo cult of scholars who yearn for the return of the golden age of pro-Indian jurisprudence and condemn the evil plenary power of Congress will analyze the period covered in this book closely with a view to whether the Indian tribes should invest their time in trying to "brief" Supreme Court nominees or, rather, to articulate coherent policy proposals for the Congress. One wonders why, in the nearly 35 years since the Jackson-Gerard era, despite the generally positive attitude of the congressional leadership on Indian policy matters, comparatively little has been accomplished and no overarching policy vision seems to guide the process.

For the Indian and Native people, one of the important lessons of this book is that one never knows when it will be in the interest of a politician or business leader to make common cause with Indian and Native interests, so it is always a good idea to leave open the possibility of a change of heart, real or cynical. We have Mark Trahant to thank for a real-life example.

Philip Sam Deloria

The Last Great Battle of the Indian Wars

It's a preposterous title: "The Last Great Battle of the Indian Wars." How can that be?

Depending on the definition, you could say the violent era of confrontation between American Indian tribes and the United States ended in southern Arizona on Jan. 10, 1915. The Yaqui people had hoped to create an independent tribal state in northern Sonora in Mexico. Tribal warriors set up a base camp in Bear Valley, helping Yaquis travel back and forth across the Mexican border for employment or supplies. The commander at Fort Sam Houston telegraphed the War Department "that a detachment of American Calvary sent into Bear Valley, twenty-five miles west of Nogales to observe trails, clashed with a band of Yaqui Indians, captured ten, one of whom died in a hospital at Nogales."

But even that was not the "last" battle. The 1960s and 1970s were a full-length chronicle of skirmishes.

Northwest tribal leaders insisted on their right to fish for salmon in the usual and accustomed places and manners as articulated by treaty. Yet state game wardens tear-gassed, beat, handcuffed and arrested traditional fishermen. The situation escalated in 1964 when treaty fishers demonstrated with a "fish-in" on Frank's Landing near Olympia, Wash. The war was on.

Hundreds of Native people were arrested and ultimately vindicated when the Supreme Court in 1979 affirmed the Boldt decision, recognizing treaty rights. Billy Frank Jr., a Nisqually leader, told The Seattle Times: "The changes in the law, the Boldt decision, never would have happened without the fish-ins. "We'd gone up to see the U.S. Attorney to get him to protect out treaty rights" without results. Something more had to be done, and, clearly, it was done.

The war metaphor is even more appropriate when considering the militancy during the late 1960s and 1970s. Boatloads of college students reclaimed Alcatraz Island on Nov. 29, 1969, and held "the Rock" for nearly two years.

The American Indian Movement later claimed the spirit of those students when the organization used the images and words of a warrior society to convey its modern rebellion. The AIM campaign included a takeover of the Bureau of Indian Affairs' headquarters in Washington, D.C., and the siege at Wounded Knee, S.D. Wounded Knee (the full story for another time) was complicated because tribal people were on both sides: Many tribal members saw their governments as reactionary. AIM to them was an inspiration and a force of justice. However, other tribal members supported their government. To the U.S. government, however, the Indian political divisions were confusing and the policy was (and is) to support the elected tribal government. So machine guns were placed in front of tribal buildings and the government did not seem to understand that it was taking a side in a civil war. But it was a war nonetheless. The U.S. Marshals called the Pentagon and it was Gen. Alexander Haig who, according to the book "Like a Hurricane," authorized the use of equipment and personnel. "The military played a central role in determining government strategy, concealing its presence with the simple yet brilliantly effective strategy of insisting that the colonels and generals sent to Pine Ridge wear civilian clothes at all times," wrote authors Paul Chaat Smith and Robert Allen Warrior.

The AIM occupation of Wounded Knee lasted for 71 days and captured the world's attention. It also helped to shape the Hollywood image of a modern warrior, still fighting for freedom. Today, movies such as "Thunderheart" celebrate that era. The film is a fictional account of a Lakota FBI agent who rediscovers his heritage and a sense of duty to his people. It is also interesting because a star of the movement, Dennis Banks, was one of the actors in the story that has loose ties to the Wounded Knee-like confrontation.

Wounded Knee was its own last battle. AIM was never again as articulate or as militant about its mission. After Wounded Knee, AIM basically became simply another Indian organization instead of a movement.

One could also accurately cite the 1975 Kootenai War in Northern Idaho as the Last Great Battle. A tiny, landless tribe sued for war against the United States by selling war bonds and collecting dime tolls from roads that passed through the reservation. After three days, the war was over – without a shot being fired. The Kootenai won and were given title to 10-plus acres for a reservation.

War, conflict and battles are part of our history, whether your point of view is that of Indian Country or the United States itself. It's a continuing history. There will always be another battle, never an end.

I think I've made the case against identifying any single event as the last great battle of the Indian wars.

Now consider this: The fight against termination and for

self-determination was unlike any other war. The consequences of defeat meant tribal people would disappear and fade into an obscure category with other hyphenated-Americans. Millions of Americans would check the census (as many do now) claiming Shoshone, Blackfeet or Cherokee heritage. But American Indians and Alaska Natives are special in the eyes of the U.S. Constitution, the national discourse – and, most important, within our own communities. That special nature was shaped by the campaign for self-determination.

At the beginning of the 20th century, mainstream American politicians hoped that American Indians would simply disappear. The only "logical" political outcome was the end of American Indian tribal cultures. It was as if the 1915 sculpture by James Fraser – The End of the Trail – had become a prescription. Or as New England poet Edna Dean Proctor wrote:

> *"And thus to bar the Red Man out,*
> *Though welcoming all other men?*
> *Nay! Let us nobly build him in,*
> *Nor rest till 'ward' and 'alien' win*
> *The rightful name of citizen!*
> *Then the reservation will be*
> *Columbia's breadth from sea to sea*
> *And Sioux, Apache, and Cheyenne*
> *Merge proudly in American!"*

Assimilation was a shared political doctrine. This was true for Democrats, Republicans and many American Indians (who wouldn't want a better education and prosperity for their children?). My own great-grandparents told my grandparents that they would be better off not speaking Indian, that they needed to learn the ways of the white people in order to succeed. Assimilation was seen by many – including American Indians – as an antidote to the bleak poverty of reservation life in the early 20th century. A 1928 policy review, now known as the Meriam Report, blamed government policies "which, if long continued, would tend to pauperize any race." The blunt assessment said Indians were poor, their health conditions were bad and the "prevailing living conditions among the great majority of the Indians are conducive to the development and spread of disease."

Yet the spirit of resistance continued as well. New leaders who formed intertribal alliances emerged to fight on Capitol Hill, in the courts and in the world of public opinion. During the late 1920s and 1930s, there was a move to reclaim independence, bolstered by the idea that tribal governments were the only ones suited to solve the problems of native people. This idea was incorporated into the Indian Reorganization Act of 1934.

But opposition to native rights also increased.

The Indian Reorganization Act was attacked from its inception. The original sponsor, Montana Sen. Burton K. Wheeler, proposed an outright repeal of the IRA only three years after its enactment. Critics said the IRA did little to assimilate American Indian people into mainstream society and instead encouraged communal thinking (the irony was that many Native leaders rejected the IRA because it did not go far enough toward self-determination).

But even the tribes that rejected the Indian Reorganization Act reconfigured their governments in new ways (and in many forms). The Navajo Nation, for example, adopted a tribal council in the 1930s. The tribe then restructured its governance in

1991, creating a three-branch system. Then in 2010 the people voted on more changes in the tribal structure, significantly reducing the size of the tribal council.

The point is that self-government, whether based on the IRA or from the broader perspective, is no longer in question. Every tribe, state and federal leader now accepts that framework as a given. Of course one reason for that is tribal religions, customs and traditions require self-government to prosper in a nation with a Judeo-Christian ethic. The same country that values the idea of the First Amendment and its establishment clause waived that principle over and over when it came to Native Americans. For example, Thomas Jefferson's effort to "civilize" American Indians was carried out by Christian missionaries as willing agents. The government hired missionaries, built church-run schools and used its resources to convert tribal people to Christianity. Even in the early 19th century, those with an appreciation for the Constitution saw the contradiction. Writer and social critic Thomas Paine warned the government to "keep a strict eye over those missionary societies, who, under the pretense of instructing the Indians, send spies into their country to find out the best lands." Later, one native religion in particular stood out as unacceptable to civilization. In the 1910s, the Indian schools began an all-out campaign to destroy the practices related to peyote. One of the federal government's boarding schools, Haskell Institute in Lawrence, Kan., even taught that freedom of religion excluded native beliefs. Peyote was evil, wrote a government teacher in a 1917 editorial in the school newspaper, The Indian Leader. "If it were true that any practice employed in religious worship can never be interfered with, there would be nothing to prevent setting up in any of our cities a pagan temple with prostitutes offering themselves in the name of religion as ministers to lust." The paper called the peyote way "a widespread evil among the Indian tribes which can be prevented only by prompt, vigorous and legislative action."

Indeed, Native religion was an impossible concept even in a country that proclaimed freedom of worship as a founding principle. Yes, Indians were free in theory to practice traditions under the First Amendment. But – and this is a huge gap in logic – how could those same ideals apply to the use of peyote? It was a drug. That translates into pure evil in the minds of school and government officials. But even beyond that: The notion of geography in religion, the importance of place, was absolutely incomprehensible to most Christian policymakers. Why couldn't Indians pray in a church like the rest of the "secular" nation? Exactly why the self-determination movement was so important to the nation – and to the evolution of American thought. No one was free to practice religion if American Indians were subject to limits on faith. Self-determination was about changing an outright hostility about native religion and culture to one ranging from either indifference or, better, acceptance.

The ultimate political expression for assimilation – and against tribal governance – was the philosophy of termination. "In everything it represented, termination threatened the very core of American Indian existence," wrote historian Donald L. Fixico in his book, "Termination and Relocation: Federal Indian Policy, 1945-1960." The idea was that the removal of American Indians from the source of their cultural existence, reservation life, would allow government obligations to evaporate. No more Indians – and no further need for a bureaucracy to effect government promises. In the span of 15 years, the government used this thinking to "terminate" some 12,000 Indians and to steal nearly 1.4 million acres of tribal land.

This is the context of the story about Henry Jackson and Forrest Gerard. There were two great battles in our era: the defeat of termination and the campaign for self-determination. First, a terrible and disastrous policy had to be rejected. Then it had to be replaced by a new and progressive policy.

Like any military campaign, the drive for self-determination was a complex enterprise in which its operations were conducted in the halls of Congress and in government offices instead of on battlefields. This last great battle redefined the nature of Indian wars in America, so much so that even the word "war" no longer has the same meaning when it is applied to the First Americans. This chapter marks the beginning of Native America as a political force, a not-so-subtle shift that meant American Indians and Alaska Natives were no longer bound by the limits of being a conquered people. Tribes were recognized as governments adding to the accepted paradigm of the city, county and state as self-governing local units. The political victories revealed in this book changed the landscape of Indian affairs so much that now virtually every member of the body politic agrees with the premise that American Indians and Alaska Natives have the right to govern themselves forever. The victories won during the last great battle have stood the test of time.

CHAPTER ONE

The Golden Era

Many American Indian legends begin with these words: "Everybody tells a different story about this." The phrase is a signal: "Pay attention! An important message is on its way." It's also a subtle clue that there are many different versions of the truth; memory is shaped by many human experiences. And because of that, sometimes, actually most of the time, a historic account may be factually correct, but it still misses a key voice. The story is not quite right.

Such is the history of "the golden era" of American Indian legislation. There is widespread recognition that the 1970s was a special time for American Indians and Alaska Natives. It was a time of convergence. There was a growing number of professional American Indians who had experience running federal programs, lobbying in Washington, D.C., and using the media to articulate their message. There were increasing Native American political forces, some modeled after the civil rights movement, others even more militant in nature. And there was a keen interest in Indian reform from the White House and Congress.

Charles Trimble, Oglala Lakota and former executive director of the National Congress of American Indians who writes a column for the national newspaper, Indian Country Today, called the 1970s "the best of times ... the most prolific era of positive national Indian policy and programs in the history of U.S.-Indian relations in the 20th century."

P. Sam Deloria, a member of the Standing Rock Sioux Tribe, and one of that early class of professional leaders, put it this way: "Indians did not discover they were Indians in the early 1970s. We were not reborn. We were simply noticed."

One measure of that notice was the difference between the 1960s and the 1970s. Both decades began with great hope. Some 700 American Indian leaders – excited by the election of President John F. Kennedy and the prospects for new beginnings – gathered in Chicago to attack termination and to articulate an alternative. "We, the Indian people, must be governed by principles in a democratic manner with a right to choose our way of life," said the 1961 Declaration of Indian Purpose. "Since our Indian culture is threatened by the presumption of being absorbed by the American society we believe we have the responsibility of preserving our precious heritage. We believe that the Indians must provide the adjustment and thus freely advance with dignity to a better life."

The declaration also included this advice for the Kennedy administration: "We believe that where programs have failed in the past, the reasons were lack of Indian understanding, planning, participation, and approval." In other words, success required Indians to be noticed.

Kennedy called the declaration a "useful reminder" that there was much work to do to improve the daily lives of American Indians. After Kennedy's assassination, President Lyndon B. Johnson's interest in American Indian issues was complicated. He did articulate a new policy approach in a message to Congress on March 6, 1968. "No enlightened nation, no responsible

Charles Trimble, then executive director of the National Congress of American Indians, at a press conference in November 1972.

government, no progressive people can sit idly by and permit this shocking situation to continue" with the Indian situation, he said. "I propose a new goal for our Indian programs: A goal that ends the old debate about 'termination' of Indian programs and stresses self-determination; a goal that erases old attitudes of paternalism and promotes partnership self-help."

That "shocking situation" had deep roots in U.S. policy. There would be phases when the government supported tribal independence, followed by a cycle of paternalism. The patterns were complicated because the three branches of government – the president, Congress and the courts – all had different approaches to dealing with the country's indigenous people. So the cycles were often not in sync – at the very moment tribes would get used to one policy approach from the Executive Branch and the Bureau of Indian Affairs, Congress would demand a new course.

Johnson attempted to set a new policy direction with a presidential proclamation. But there was no action. There were no calls from the White House to key congressional leaders. It was as if a single paper signed by the president could substitute for decades of legislative history and action.

In terms of the actual words used, Johnson's message was similar to one announced by President Richard M. Nixon just two years later. But Nixon's July 8, 1970, message proclaiming "self-determination without termination" came at exactly the right moment. Nixon was moving with Congress and the country as a whole. America was ready to settle the disputes about the nature of tribal sovereignty and to enact self-determination as the law of the land. Indeed, the idea of self-determination took hold because it defined a new era. There was a convergence of events and people, each being noticed, and each with a new story to tell.

Two of those stories belong to Henry M. "Scoop" Jackson and Forrest J. Gerard. The partnership between Jackson and Gerard "launched the most productive period in the history of federal legislation dealing with American Indians and Alaska Native affairs," said Deloria, who is now director of the Ameri-

UNIVERSITY OF WASHINGTON LIBRARIES, SPECIAL COLLECTIONS, UW19599

Henry M. Jackson chairs a hearing of the U.S. Senate's Interior and Insular Affairs Committee, ca. 1960s.

can Indian Graduate Center in Albuquerque (a national organization that provides scholarships and other educational assistance to Native Americans). Their work put the polices of tribal self-determination into "concrete" form, laying the groundwork for "spectacular progress made by federally-recognized tribes in the intervening years, none of which would have been possible without their understanding of the fundamental restructuring that would be required."

Scoop's legacy is already well known and etched in the nation's memory. He is remembered for his work as a champion of America's international face as well as one of the architects of the country's environmental policies. A closer read of his body of legislation and his legacy on American Indian policy comes through clearly. As chairman of the Senate's Interior Committee, Jackson's name could have claimed authorship for every piece of Indian legislation that sailed through Congress during those best of times. It could have been the Jackson Indian health bill or the Jackson Indian self-determination law. But that wasn't Jackson's style.

On the other hand, credit is rarely given to a member of a senator's staff for the boss's legislation. That's just not done. Anonymity is part of the deal when one works on Capitol Hill. It's always the senator's idea, the senator's bill and the senator's influence on history. That, too, was Forrest Gerard's style.

Early on, Gerard learned – and accepted – the unofficial set of rules for staff on Capitol Hill. Successful staff members let their boss get all the credit – and are eager to accept blame when things go wrong. That's the requirement for any professional who wants to be effective in politics.

But what works on Capitol Hill doesn't accurately tell the story. Forrest Gerard was the first American Indian to be in a position to design, write, shepherd and do whatever was required to move American Indian legislation through Congress. That's why the history of this country would be incomplete unless one recognizes both men and their partnership.

"The story of Jackson's conversion is the story of Forrest Gerard and his relationship with Jackson," said Dr. Abe Bergman, a Seattle pediatrician. Bergman once called his practice "political medicine" because he spent so much time trying to improve public health through legislation. He worked with both Jackson and Gerard on health legislation.

"I want Forrest Gerard to be honored in Indian Country. I don't think Indians have any idea what this man did. And it's because he's so self-effacing and because he's so dedicated ... he just did incredible things for Indian history."

National Congress of American Indians President Mel Tonasket gives an award to Rep. Morris Udall, D-Arizona, and Sen. Henry M. Jackson at a special banquet in Washington.

Gerard was ideally suited for both his era and the mission. He had experience working for Indian programs in a variety of federal agencies and had been a Congressional Fellow in both House and Senate offices. He was a member of Montana's Blackfeet Tribe and had grown up on the reservation.

"He brought to the job the knowledge instilled by years of working with tribal governments and the governmental agencies serving them," Sam Deloria said. "Too often, the otherwise capable congressional staff members lacked personal knowledge of the people, communities and organizations affected by proposed legislation, and lacked the knowledge of the actual workings of the federal agencies responsible for implementation of legislation, particularly legislation that makes far-reaching structural changes."

That legislative record speaks for itself.

"Some of the legislation which bears Gerard's imprint includes such things as the Indian Health Care Improvement Act, the Indian Self-Determination and Education Assistance Act, the Indian Finance Act, the Sub-Marginal Lands Act, and many, many others," said Lee Metcalf, Montana's U.S. senator from 1961 through 1978.

Metcalf's words treat Gerard with the respect of a colleague, a notion shared by many on Capitol Hill. History rarely records the staff members who carry out the work of legislators. After all, it is the senator's name on the bill and the senator made the appropriate argument during the actual debate. But no senator, not a single one, has ever been successful without talented people moving a bill forward one step at a time.

"Just as a dozen Washington insiders of that era have laid claim to sole authorship of the famous Nixon Indian Message to Congress that presaged the deluge of legislation, so too do many people and organizations make claim to responsibility for the positive policy of that era," wrote Trimble in the newspaper, Indian Country Today. "But from what I have seen, as executive director of the National Congress of American Indians through much of the 1970s, without unsung heroes like Forrest Gerard in key positions on Capitol Hill, much of that would not have come about in the fashion that it did. Gerard did great work – subtly, without fanfare, and too often without recognition or even thanks. His approach was honesty and directness in dealing with Indian Country, and he never wavered in his loyalty to the tribes."

Jackson's loyalty and history was another matter.

The National Congress of American Indians' honored Jackson at a dinner on June 25, 1975. It was the 99th anniversary of the "Custer battle." The program cover was a cartoon by Pat Oliphant. "Scoop" sat on a horse alongside Gen. George Armstrong Custer. "Don't worry," Custer says. "The Indians want to honor us."

It was a subtle joke.

"Sen. Jackson was chosen for the award because of his sponsorship of the Indian Finance Act, the Indian Self-Determination Act, both of which passed the Congress in 1974, and for his sponsorship of the Indian Health Care Improvement Act, which has recently been passed unanimously by the Senate," wrote Trimble, who was then NCAI's executive director. "All three bills are key pieces of legislation for Indian communities and provide a good basis for the advancement of Indian people."

But that's exactly the point of the joke and what made the night exciting. This was the same Henry Jackson who had once been dismissed by some as a modern ally of Custer. In his role as chairman of the powerful Senate Interior Committee, Jackson had long advocated for "the disastrous policy of termination."

Only five years before the NCAI dinner, that same phrase – "the disastrous policy of termination" – was a chapter in Vine Deloria Jr.'s best-selling book, "Custer Died For Your Sins."

Deloria wrote that people shouldn't feel guilty about their ancestors killing off Indians when the U.S. Congress was engaged in "a more devious" attack on Indian communities by terminating federal services. He called it the single most critical issue facing American Indians and blamed Chairman Jackson and his committee staffer, James Gamble.

"This policy was not conceived as a policy of murder," Deloria wrote. "Rather it was thought that it would provide the elusive 'answer' to the Indian problem. And when it proved to be no answer at all, Congress continued its policy ...."

But Congress did change its mind – a shift that occurred

because the country was changing in so many ways during the upheavals generated by the civil rights movement. At the same time, Jackson was rethinking his approach and policies.

Jackson wanted a new approach on Indian issues and that's why he needed someone who had the confidence of tribal leaders, someone who could also be trusted and a complete Capitol Hill professional. This matched Jackson's own sense of professionalism. He had a reputation in Washington as a smart senator who understood the nature and complexity of policy issues.

"If you've been in government a long time, as I have been, then the most exciting thing you encounter in government is competence. Why is this exciting? Because it's rare," boomed Sen. Daniel Patrick Moynihan when endorsing Jackson for the 1976 presidential nomination. "If you think there is anything dull about a man who knows as much, who's done as much, and who has moved as much forward in government, when the opposite is almost always the case. This man knows his business."

Barry Dunsmore of ABC News was less kind. "Scoop could put people to sleep like no other politician. He was good one-on-one, good on talk shows, but he could not stir up a crowd."

Jackson described himself as "a different kind" of politician and a "different kind of Democrat." When running for the 1972 presidential nomination, he described his philosophy this way: "I call myself a liberal. Some people say I am too liberal. Some say I am too conservative. If that makes me a middle-of-the-roader, that's all right with me."

In a 1976 interview, Jackson said people want more integrity from their leaders. "Well, I think above all, they want from their officials a straightforward answer," he said. "I think they're crying out for officials who will speak straight from the shoulder and tell them like it is even though the person listening to the speaker will disagree with them. They want a frank and direct answer. They want the truth."

President Ronald Reagan, less than a year after the senator's death, called Jackson "one of the greatest lawmakers of our century. He helped to build the community of democracies and worked tirelessly to keep it vigorous and secure. He pioneered in the preservation of the nation's natural heritage, and he embodied integrity and decency in the profession of politics."

Reagan awarded the Presidential Medal of Freedom to Jackson's family on June 26, 1984, as a testimony to his legacy. The president cited the senator's long record in "the making of a noble foreign policy: a love of freedom; a will to defend it; and the knowledge that America could not and must not attempt to float along alone, a blissful island of democracy in a sea of totalitarianism." During the White House ceremony, Reagan captured Jackson's unique role in history, both in terms of foreign policy and the environment. He also reflected Scoop's nature as a person. "Scoop Jackson was a serious man — not somber or self-important, but steady and solemn," Reagan said. "He didn't think much of the cosmetics of politics. He wasn't interested in image. He was a practitioner of the art of politics, and he was a personage in the affairs of the world. But there was no cause too great or too small for his attention."

One missing element from the Medal of Freedom citation was Scoop's record on American Indian and Alaska Native issues. Nixon articulated self-determination and the rejection of termination, but it was Jackson and Gerard who made the president's policy the law of the land.

Everybody tells a different story about this era. But this account goes behind the scenes and reproduces the voices and personalities that for too long have been missing from history.

CHAPTER TWO

Quieting Termination

The story of Henry M. Jackson and termination cannot be effectively communicated if you start at the beginning. This happened, then this, then that, is a narrative form that doesn't work in this instance. To understand what "termination" means to Native Americans you have to start with the consequences, a failure so great that its ghosts haunt even the current thinking of tribal leaders. The phrase, "another termination effort" is as lethal in the 21st century as it was in the 20th century; so much so that many innovations disappear as quickly as they are announced because the opposition raises the specter of termination. Why is this collective memory so powerful? Simple. It is the 20th century's version of the Indian wars, with battles fought in a political context. Even the word "terminate" carries allusions of war, death and destruction. The policy implemented the horrible idea that a good Indian was a dead Indian, that the culture had to be killed to save the person.

The drama of termination was supposed to follow this script: Members of a resource-rich tribe were to be convinced they would do better on their own – and could vote to liquidate their own tribal government. After a "yes" vote – by hook or crook – money was paid for an undervalued asset, such as timber, and the proceeds divided equally. After the money disappeared, the social ills remained and neither the state nor county governments were equipped to respond.

The context of termination – especially to American Indian people – is critical to understanding Jackson's role.

But it is also important to note that he was not alone; the context for termination fit the era. As historian S. Lyman Tyler put it in his 1964 history of termination: It was "a period of trying new approaches." First Congress recognized and supported tribal governments under the framework of the Indian Reorganization Act of 1934. That law was supposed to return democratic power to tribes to make their own decisions about the future (although with the Bureau of Indian Affairs acting as the executive branch, including the power to veto tribal laws). But even that went too far for some in Congress. Only three years after the IRA's enactment, six bills pressed for the repeal of the IRA, including one from the original sponsor, Sen. Burton Wheeler, a Democrat from Montana.

Congress was shifting gears because of a general greed for Indian resources plus the distaste for anything different, including tribal cultures.

"People (were) interested in the property reserved to the Indians," Tyler wrote. Tribal communities were seen as communist, anti-Christian and outside the American definition of normal.

Currently, it's easy to condemn termination. We know the policy was a disaster and, therefore, everyone involved must have been evil.

But the record shows a range of logic. Many truly believed that the best course was to assimilate American Indians into the rest of the country, while critics resented appropriating any extra dollars for a distinct population. On top of that grid there were those who were eager to rip off land, timber or other natural resources controlled by tribal communities.

Jackson was elected to the House as a fresh face in the Roosevelt sweep of 1940. He was 28 years old – one newspaper referred to him as the "baby of the 77th Congress." Soon after, as a representative from a Western state, Jackson found himself engaged with American Indian policy issues.

"I have about as few Indians in my district as any district in the country; probably no more than 2,000 or 3,000 in the entire district," Jackson said a few years later in a floor speech. Yet, he continued that he had given a lot of thought to the complicated nature of Indian law and the importance of settling land claims.

Both the Democratic and Republican parties in 1940 had formally called for a final settlement of Indian claims against the United States. Tribes and the National Congress of American Indians eagerly supported this initiative as a matter of basic fairness. Jackson became chairman of the House Indian Affairs Committee in 1944 and a year later held hearings across the country to build a legislative record for settling those claims. The Washington Democrat argued that American Indians needed a fair resolution before there could be a new national American Indian policy. He was particularly troubled by the dual nature of the legal status of individual American Indians.

"Today, any white man who has supplied goods or services to the United States under contract, may, if the United States has failed to carry out its part of the bargain, go into a Court of Claims, or in certain entities, into the Federal District Court, and secure a full, free and fair hearing on his claims against the government," Jackson said on Dec. 26, 1945. "This is an integral part of the American system of justice under which the humblest citizen, and the highest official, are equal before the law. The only American citizen today who is denied such a recourse to the courts is the Indian."

Jackson wanted to make certain that the system was fair, based on a sound legal process and the rights of the individual, instead of a system focused only on tribal community rights. "People of Indian blood who are fully capable of taking their place in non-reservation life on the same basis as any other citizen are impelled to cling to tribal associations because of the fear that separation from the tribe might deprive him of a share of a settlement which he believes the government may some day make," Jackson's committee report said. Only the Truman administration, however, feared that claim settlements could be greater than the government could afford in a nation already burdened by the cost of World War II.

Jackson was clear about what he wanted from the settlement process. During a May 20, 1946, congressional debate about resolving tribal claims, Jackson said it was essential that American Indians be able to proceed under the rule of law. If that did happen, only then could the federal government consider ending its trusteeship and financial obligations.

"I realize that the subject is a complicated one," Jackson said. "I might even say, a forbidding one – to those who have not given it much time and thought." And that thought, for Jackson, meant a concentration on the claims resolution. "Let us pay up our debts," Jackson said. "Let us pay up our debts to the Indian tribes that sold us the land that we live on. They sold it for little enough, generally a few cents an acre. Let us pay at least what we promised to pay, if we have already not done so, and let us see that the Indians have their fair day in court so that they can call the various government agencies to account on the obligations that the federal government assumed. And let us make sure that when the Indians have their day in court they have an opportunity to present all their claims of every kind, shape, and variety, so that this problem can be solved once and for all without coming back to haunt us or our successors …."

The intent was to resolve two centuries of property rights' and then settle the debt with the original owners, Indian people. The benefit for the federal government was resolution; the belief that this would end the idea that the country was stolen from the Indians because any claims to aboriginal title would be extinguished and the Indians compensated.

The House bill called for a strict five-year time limit to resolve claims. "When we set up a Court of Private Land Claims in California in 1851," Jackson said, "we set a limit of 2 years on the presentation of Spanish and Mexican claims. We cleared up that situation in that period of time … I think we can expect finality in the work of the Indian Claims Commission."

That finality was the foundation of termination. "I think that as long as these claims remain unsettled and until some final disposition is made, we are going to continue on indefinitely. It is getting worse every year," Jackson said. "A lot of the Indians have gone on to school and graduated, but they come back to the reservation to live there. Why? Because they feel that if they leave and lose their enrollment status they will not be able to participate in their ancestral claim if it is settled, so they go back to the reservation."

In that same debate, Jackson raised a rhetorical question: "Is it not true, may I say to the gentleman from South Dakota, that it costs more to take care of the Indians in the United States than it costs to operate the legislative branch of the government?"

After a quick "yes" from Rep. Karl Mundt, the Republican from South Dakota, Jackson said the BIA cost taxpayers $26 million a year.

Mundt picked up Jackson's cost example and continued with that theme: "We have been appropriating funds for Indian administration at least since 1775, when Benjamin Franklin, Patrick Henry and James Wilson were appointed Indian Commissioners by the Continental Congress. For 170 years the total of our annual appropriations for this purpose has been growing. Today our Indian population is increasing twice as rapidly as our white population. Unless we do something to reach a fair, just, and permanent solution to the Indian problem, that will incorporate the Indian into our national economy, we are going to have to look forward to spending increasing millions every year on Indian administration. That would be the inevitable result of a 'do-nothing' policy."

Jackson and the House Indian Affairs Committee saw the claims as the method to "settle this Indian problem in the United States. We are appropriating $30,000,000 a year to the Indian service, trying to take care of the Indians on a paternalistic basis and the result is that as long as these claims are pending, the Indians will stay on the reservations and never want to leave, and it simply means more cost to the government, and from an economic standpoint we have come to the conclusion that this is about the only solution."

In hindsight, it's interesting that Jackson placed so much hope on the claims process since it was flawed from the beginning. Congress and the Truman administration wanted the finality of the claims – but there was no incentive to pay the true cost. The purchase of land titles (plus interest) would amount to hundreds of millions of dollars. The government hoped to pay a fraction of that – and even then failed to appropriate the promised funds. You could make the case that ending paternalism made sense – except it was just a ruse to evade financial responsibility.

Still, the National Congress of American Indians and many tribes actively lobbied for the president's signature for the creation of an Indian Claims Commission. Secretary of Interior Julius Krug supported the bill because it would give tribes the resources to manage their own affairs with fewer federal dollars. Despite the fact that he, Mundt and Jackson all expected that future appropriations for Indian programs would be cut based on the price of a settlement. Mundt said resolving the claims would allow Indians to act as "self-respecting citizens instead of puppets of an endless bureaucracy."

President Truman signed the claims legislation on Aug. 13, 1946, predicting a new era for American Indians. "They had proved their loyalty during World War II the wisdom of a national policy built on the principle of fair dealing. The president hoped that a final claims settlement would encourage Indians to find community in the nation instead of the tribe and to fully share in the prosperity of America's postwar capitalist market economy," wrote historian Kenneth R. Philip in his book "Termination Revisited."

The problem with this imposing idea was its execution. Truman's appointments for the Indian Claims Commission were men with absolutely no experience in either history or tribal issues. The commission dismissed some of the early claims without even bothering to hear any evidence.

"Once it became clear that awards would be dismissed, delayed, or smaller than expected, the U.S. government encountered growing criticism from Indians," Phillip wrote, "the promise of self-determination was broken when Congress withheld final claims payments."

Meanwhile, the government began to implement the other phase in the claims bargain, termination.

Assistant Secretary of the Interior William E. Warne put it this way on Jan. 6, 1948: "The avowed objective of the Indian Service of the Department of Interior through the years has been to work itself out of a job. Within the last year the committees of Congress, which are concerned with Indian affairs, have expressed some doubts whether the controls were being released rapidly enough. To reaffirm this policy of releasing Indians from government supervision, the Congress made substantial reductions in funds appropriated for this fiscal year for Indian administration at all levels of the service."

The government started with a list of tribes "ready" for termination. Acting BIA Commissioner William Zimmerman divided 378,000 Native Americans into three groups: "Predominately acculturated," including the Flathead in Montana and Menominee in Wisconsin; "semi-acculturated" groups such as the Cherokee in Oklahoma and the Warm Springs' bands in Oregon; and finally, the "predominately Indian populations" from more isolated reservations such as Pine Ridge, South Dakota.

"The objective of the program should be the eventual discharge of the federal government's obligation, legal, moral, or otherwise, and the discontinuance of federal supervision and control at the earliest possible date compatible with the government's trust responsibility," Zimmerman wrote on May 28, 1948. "This may mean early termination of all federal supervision for some groups, whereas for others it seems obvious that certain federal activities, including the development of resources, must be continued for many years."

Congress cited Zimmerman and other BIA reports as evidence for its enactment of House Concurrent Resolution 108 on Aug. 1, 1958. That measure described the policy of Congress "as rapidly as possible, to make the Indians within the territorial limits of the United States subject to the same laws and entitled to the same privileges and responsibilities as are applicable to other citizens of the United States, and to end their status as wards of the United States, and to grant them all of the rights and prerogatives pertaining to American citizenship."

Jackson, who had since been elected to the Senate from Washington, was the sponsor of the companion to HCR 108 in the upper chamber.

That resolution was the legislative trigger for the government to terminate reservations – and at the top of the list was the Menominee Tribe of Wisconsin. The first step to make it happen was a BIA promise to resolve land claims quickly so each individual member could receive a check for $1,500 (a figure that would be worth more than 10 times that amount at today's prices).

"In the beginning, it was the desire of the tribe to ask for the use of some of its funds in the form of a per capita payment," the Menominee News wrote on March 23, 1956. "This request was honored by the House of Representatives and passed on to the United States Senate. Upon reaching the Committee on Interior and Insular Affairs, the Chairman of the Committee, the Honorable Arthur V. Watkins, seized upon this simple bill and attached thirteen amendments which had the effect of terminating the Menominee Indian Tribe from federal supervision without consultation and consent of the Menominee Indian people themselves. This became a long drawn-out fight between the tribe and the United States Senate to that end that the tribe was in no position to properly stand off some of the mandates."

Watkins was explicit: Termination was the price for any claims settlement. Philleo Nash, the lieutenant governor of Wisconsin at the time, called it "involuntary termination" because the "Menominee people did not want termination. Consent to termination was wrested from the tribe under threat to pay the monies awarded the tribe in a successful litigation under the Indian Claims Act."

If Jackson's endorsement for the claims process and termination was about ending paternalism, then Arthur Watkins' support stemmed from his general disdain for government. He particularly objected to the idea that the United States had any treaty obligations. He said Indians "want all the benefits of the things we have – highways, schools, hospitals, everything that civilization furnished – but they don't want to help pay their share of it."

Joseph Garry, from Idaho's Coeur d'Alene Reservation and president of the National Congress of American Indians, told delegates at the 1958 convention that Congress had adopted the termination resolution in good faith "believing it would be good for Indian people" but it was clearly dangerous and a disaster. He called for tribes to work together for a new policy, "the reverse of 108."

By 1958, the NCAI had picked up important congressional allies: Rep. Lee Metcalf, a Democrat from Montana, and at least tacit support from Washington's senior Democratic senator, Warren Magnuson. Metcalf told the NCAI convention that he was going to go to war over the government's termination policy. "Our first job in the next session will be to adopt a sound declaration of policy in the Indian field, wiping out the concurrent resolution on which most of the so-called 'termination' pressure has been based," he said.

Frank George, a Nez Perce who was a member of the Colville Confederated Tribes from Washington and a delegate to the Democratic National Convention in 1960, framed termination as a Republican and Eisenhower administration policy. "The fact remains that the Indian Bureau field personnel and the Washington staff devote considerable time in planting ideas in the minds of the general public and even tribal governing bodies that the solution to the problems of the American Indians is the termination of federal trusteeship." George made the case for a post-termination policy, based on leveraging tribal assets and better education opportunities.

Robert Yellowtail, a Republican and the former superintendent at Crow Agency, dismissed both political parties' efforts. "Indians were lucky to come out with their shirts under the policy of liquidation," he said. Nonetheless Yellowtail favored Nixon because he thought the then vice president would shake-up the BIA establishment.

Back in their home state, both Jackson and Magnuson had pressured the Colville Tribes toward termination. Several Colville termination bills had been introduced, beginning with a 1955 resolution. Jackson's termination proposal had passed the Senate several times, but never the House.

The Senate Interior Committee was not only on record supporting termination, but its members pressed for explanations about the slow implementation. "The Committee is deeply concerned about the failure of the Bureau of Indian Affairs to carry out the intent of House Concurrent Resolution 108 ... programs for tribes, many of whom were reported by the Bureau itself as being ready for termination legislation more than ten years ago," a committee statement said in April 1964.

And the Colvilles were one of those "ready" tribes. The situation was supposed to be resolved because of the perception of a significant support for termination among the Colville membership, partly because of the potential for large per-capita payment.

The tribal governing body and its chairman Narcisse Nicholson Jr. blamed Congress for the delays. "You may be sure that I will continue to do everything possible to advance consideration of the Colville termination bill in this Congress," Washington Rep. Tom Foley wrote the chairman in 1969.

Congress had ordered the Colvilles to develop a five-year termination plan in 1965 in exchange for clear title to reservation land. Three years later the Colville Business Council polled tribal members with this question: "Do you favor termination and liquidation of the tribal owned reservation assets at a fair value with the proceeds distributed equally to the members of the tribes?" The result was one-sided: More than two-thirds of the membership approved. Who would not want the money?

Chairman Nicholson argued that the Colville tribe should end its relationship with the BIA because "with only a relatively few exceptions, the tribal families of today are self-supporting." He added, "Lack of employment, to the degree that it exists, is largely due to character faults which cannot be cured by paternalism."

In Washington, D.C., BIA Commissioner Robert L. Bennett said that even though he was personally opposed to termination, he would "honor and carry out any decisions that are made by the people of the tribe, whether or not this may be in agreement or disagreement with what may happen to be particular policy of the bureau."

However, Lucy Covington represented the minority voice on the Colville Business Council, along with Shirley Palmer. Covington led a steady campaign to quiet what she termed "the present fever and fervor for termination." She published Our Heritage, a newspaper reminding tribal members what was at stake. The newspaper profiled candidates opposed to termination and reported on recent lobbying efforts to stop termination bills. She called the council's polls bogus because they did not address the manner of termination. Nor did the polls ask non-resident tribal members for their opinion.

Another approach, a partition of the reservation, was met with equal opposition. Covington called that alternative a disguised "sale of the reservation." At a reservation rally before the tribal election, author Vine Deloria Jr. told tribal members: "You will never be paid anything near what your reservation is worth." But supporters of termination cited a Stanford Research Institute study that estimated each member's net worth from tribal assets at $30,000 (worth more than $160,000 by today's standards). Our Heritage, in a cartoon drawn by Charles Trimble, framed the money-versus-land issue in three images. One panel showed a welfare agent telling a Colville mother: "I'm sorry we can't do anything for you. Why don't you go back to your reservation." She responds: "We don't have anyplace to go. Our grandfathers sold our reservation." The second panel shows another mother in front of a nice house "on the land our grandfather saved for us. We get a check for our timber rights, too!" The third panel shows a coin flying away, with the words: "Money has its own death song. Money doesn't last long. It only flies away. Only the land and mountains are forever!"

By 1970 termination looked like a done deal. Foley introduced his termination proposal in the House with Jackson adding a companion bill in the Senate. The only roadblock was a May tribal election with a slate of "Indian Rights" candidates, Clarence Desautel, Mel Tonasket, Andrew Joseph, Donald Carson and Covington.

"I have been elected several times to the Colville Business Council and my record shows that I have been against termination – the giving up of Indian rights, the selling out of Indian lands from Indian ownership. In fighting the termination bills, I have worked against the strategy of misleading opinion polls, against inaccurate promises to Indian people and against an inert majority on the council," Covington wrote in Our Heritage. "It is sad to look back on our own Colville reservation and see an inert Council trying to starve its people into submission. ... Vote for the candidates of the Committee on Indian Rights of the Colville Indian Reservation."

The campaign was a success. On May 8, 1971, Covington's allies were elected to the council. Nicholson was defeated in his district, Omak, and was replaced by a council member who was opposed to termination. Mel Tonasket, only 30 years old, was elected chairman. The new business council called for more federal support, closed a reservation lake to outsiders and voted to take back law enforcement powers that had been ceded to the state of Washington.

Jackson had been moving away from his support of termination. There was no single message identifying Jackson's opposition to termination – and the record shows more of an evolution than an epiphany. For example, his letters to Chairman Nicholson had become almost perfunctory by 1970: "Senator Magnuson and I have sponsored the measure by request, and copies of S. 3518 are enclosed for your information and use." There was not the same sort of language promising quick action.

More important, some three months before the Colville election ended the tribe's political support for termination, Jackson had hired Forrest J. Gerard as his primary agent on Indian affairs for the Senate Interior and Insular Affairs Committee. Gerard had been clear during his hiring process: He wasn't willing to take the job if it only meant pursuing the policies of termination. But Jackson was clearly ready to lead the committee in a new direction.

Jackson even promised tribal leaders "a far-reaching review of Indian programs during the 92nd Congress." In a February 1971 story in the Colville's Tribal Tribune, Jackson said this kind of review was essential "because of the almost overwhelming social, economic and legal complexities which Indian people encounter in seeking solutions to their problems. These complexities evolved because of the unique historical legal relationship of the Indian people with the federal government."

CHAPTER THREE

The Gentlemen's Club Versus Blue Lake

New Mexico's Clinton P. Anderson thought the Senate would treat him with deference after his election in 1948. He was, after all, a former member of the House of Representatives and Secretary of Agriculture. "But I quickly ran head-on into the men who governed the Senate, and I learned that I was as naïve as I had been as a freshmen in the House," Anderson wrote in his memoir.

The Gentlemen's Club was in "a transitional state." Anderson said Sen. Clyde Hoey, a Democrat from North Carolina, was the last to wear winged-collars and a long swallowtail coat. "It wasn't the clothes so much that made the old Senate as the feeling which wearing the clothes conveyed. It embodied an orthodoxy which demanded of newcomers that they make their beginning years an apprenticeship for great responsibility," Anderson wrote. This was the era when the Senate was all male and the age of 60 was considered a "fine time" to begin a career. The enforcement of that Senate orthodoxy was by long-serving members from the South. The most powerful of those, Dick Russell of Georgia, said those rules were designed to protect what they considered their "Southern way of life." Before the transition, the South could block civil rights legislation – or anything else that its regional caucus opposed. It was the same philosophy that governed the Committee on Interior and Insular Affairs. This was the one assignment that was the exclusive perquisite of Westerners, designed to protect the Western way of life.

"It is in the West where lie the largest tracts of public lands, the biggest Indian reservations, most of the mining of metals, the giant reclamation projects, the extensive lumbering operations," Anderson wrote. "The businessmen involved in these matters keep a great deal of pressure on the committee and they have always had many friends among its members." The friends of the Gentlemen's Club included the American Mining Congress, the United Mine Workers, ranchers and Western state politicians.

On the House side, Anderson's counterpart was Wayne Aspinall, the Democrat from Colorado. He complained "that his house Interior Committee was far different in composition from its Senate counterpart," according to the Senate's official historian, Richard Allen Baker, in the book, "Conservation Politics." "States east of the Mississippi River were represented on the panel and their interests were often at odds with those of the western-dominated Senate committee."

American Indians were the beneficiary – if that's the right word – of much attention from those Western-specific interests. Chairman Anderson once recalled a Pueblo leader's view of a complicated wilderness bill. "When toward the end of the day," Anderson wrote, "the Indian's turn came, he rose with great dignity and thanked us for safeguarding his people's land. Then referring to the jurisdictional disputes over administration proposed law, he said he had a simple solution: 'Just give it back to the Indians.' I recognized that we couldn't rectify centuries of injustice toward the Indian by accepting his suggestion, but I

Senate Interior Committee Chairman Henry M. Jackson (center), his daughter, Anna Marie, his mentor New Mexico Sen. Clinton P. Anderson, Alaska Sen. Ernest Gruening and Idaho Sen. Len B. Jordan.

did believe we had an obligation not to make matters worse."

Anderson said what he meant when it came to returning land to American Indians, but his words fell short on his obligation not to make matters worse. Anderson was, as one historian put it, one of the "guardians" of the termination policy. He was a willing Democratic ally when Republican Arthur Watkins of Utah chaired the committee and coerced tribes into termination. Even though the Democrats were back in charge, Chairman Anderson was determined to stick with the termination policy.

Henry M. Jackson was Anderson's protégé, a smart, hard-working young, up-and-coming senator. Then in 1963, there was an unexpected leadership vacancy: Oklahoma Sen. Robert Kerr died, opening up the chairmanship of the Senate Aeronautical and Space Sciences Committee. This was a post once held by Lyndon B. Johnson. LBJ and Anderson "both appreciated the benefit of raw, naked power from pouring money back into their home states and were artists at it," said Bill Van Ness, who was Jackson's chief counsel for the Interior Committee. "Lyndon called him up and said, 'Clint, I want you to go over and take the chairmanship of the space committee.' … but that meant he had to give up the chairmanship of the Interior Committee. Clint really didn't want to give it up. He liked the western stuff, especially loved the position of power on the water and power subcommittee where he could keep water flowing to New Mexico. But eventually he did it and New Mexico and Texas would split up the benefits of the space program."

Richard Baker wrote that Anderson was "giving up little" because "his influence with committee colleagues was not likely to diminish. This was evident in the forthcoming decision to retain Jerry Verkler as committee staff director. Verkler had come to the post from Anderson's personal staff."

Van Ness said the deal was that Jackson would protect Anderson's staff on the committee – and that included James Gamble, who was the principal point person on American Indian issues and a fervent advocate for termination.

A few years later, Vine Deloria Jr. summed up the view from Indian Country of Anderson, Jackson and Gamble in "Custer Died For Your Sins": "With the advent of the War on Poverty the push for termination has slowed, but certainly not stopped. Chief advocate of termination is James Gamble, staff member of the Senate Interior Committee, which is the parent committee of the Indian subcommittee. Gamble has remained in the background while Henry Jackson, chairman of the committee, has had to accept public responsibility for Gamble's moves against the tribes. Rarely does a judgment bill come before the committee but what Gamble tries to have a termination rider attached. So powerful is Gamble that Jackson might be characterized as his front man. But Jackson is busy with his work on Foreign Relations and other important committees and so he accepts Gamble's recommendations without much consideration of alternatives."

No issue better illustrated the transition state of the Interior Committee than that of the Taos Pueblo demand for the return of Blue Lake in New Mexico. This issue broke all the rules of Senate protocol because it questioned a senator's absolute prerogative in his home state and a committee chairman's authority over an issue within his jurisdiction.

The Taos Pueblos had been seeking their sacred Blue Lake since President Teddy Roosevelt declared the lake part of the Kit Carson National Forest in 1906. In 1965 the Indian Claims Commission declared that the Pueblo had aboriginal ownership of some 130,000 acres – including the City of Taos – that had been stolen over the centuries under both Spanish and U.S. rule. Normally the government paid money only when it settled and extinguished title claims. But the Pueblos insisted that any settlement had to include the return of Blue Lake. "The 48,000-acre Blue Lake area is the 'natural cathedral' of the Taos people, filled with many religious shrines," said a story in the NCAI Bulletin. The church metaphor is an understatement: Taos people believe their ancestors emerged from the depths of the lake and its waters are the inner-sanctum of the temple where ceremonies are conducted throughout the year.

Anderson had been in charge of the forest service as Secretary of Agriculture during the Truman administration and this issue was from his home state of New Mexico. Anderson introduced legislation to return the land in 1966, but he made clear that he was doing so only as a courtesy to his constituents; in fact he remained opposed to any return of land.

Two years later, the U.S. House of Representatives passed a bill to transfer the lands back to the Interior Department and Taos Pueblo control. But the Senate remained an obstacle. At a Senate hearing, Anderson repeated the Forest Service's main argument: "This is a wilderness area and wilderness once locked up should not be unlocked, it should be as God left it."

Jackson agreed. "We are concerned that the transfer of the land in trust or by outright conveyance regardless of the acreage involved would be a far-reaching undesirable precedent," he said. Later, Jackson escalated that warning, calling the precedent "dangerous."

The Senate was not going to move this legislation forward. The New Mexico Review and Legislative Journal in Santa Fe said in November 1969: "Opposition to the plan is small but powerful, Sen. Clinton P. Anderson of New Mexico, while not opposed to giving the Indians back their shrine, is unwilling to give them surrounding land."

Anderson responded: "I want to make sure that the Indians are protected, but I do not believe that they need to have a deed to the land to have this guarantee. In testimony before the Senate Interior Committee they were unable to give even one example of anyone disturbing their worship or desecrating their shrines."

But, as the New Mexico Review pointed out, even that statement was misleading. "Their 'shines' include the whole 48,000 acres – not only Blue Lake and its immediate vicinity, but land between Blue Lake and the Pueblo. And as for having their worship disturbed or 'desecrated,' the whole history of their dealings with the Forest Service has been one desecration from another."

The concept of the Forest Service and the multiple use of public lands for recreation, timber and ranching was foreign to the Pueblo way of thinking. "Indians want to stop commercial exploitation of land that they consider their 'church.' But timber and recreational interests have powerful lobbies," the New Mexico Review said.

While Anderson had been successful killing the Blue Lake legislation in 1966 and 1968, there was growing pressure in the 91st Congress to resolve the claims. The New Mexican, Santa Fe's daily newspaper, said the "Taos case has become celebrated in the nation with many feeling their cause stands for religious freedom and justice for Indians."

Secretary of the Interior Walter Hickel testified in 1969 that no claim against the government was more compelling than that of Taos. The secretary wrote Anderson that a full return of the land was the only way to protect the Pueblo's religious freedom.

House Interior Committee Chairman Aspinall agreed. "This land is vital to the continued welfare of Indians, particularly the protection of their religion," he said.

Even New Mexico Gov. David Cargo, a Republican, was in favor of the legislation. He told the Albuquerque Journal it was a "righteous claim" and that "the White Man ought to be embracing Indian citizens instead of denying them their rights." He promised to lobby the Nixon administration to support the bill.

The Nixon White House had been silent. One tribal newspaper feared it was possible that the House and Senate could finally pass the Blue Lake bill only to have it vetoed by the president because of its cost. Yet, according to John Ehrlichman, the president's assistant for domestic affairs, this was an issue where the administration wanted to find a way to do the right thing.

The problem was Chairman Jackson.

Nixon was fond of Jackson and saw him as an ally on many international issues, such as the Anti-Ballistic Missile Treaty with the Soviet Union. Within the White House there was concern that Jackson would vote against the treaty if Nixon became his opponent on the Blue Lake issue. According to historian R.C. Gordon-McCutchan, in his book, "The Taos Indians and the Battle for Blue Lake," Anderson warned the White House that supporting the Pueblo would be a "serious mistake." Jackson told the White House bluntly, "We have to decide whether it is ABM, or whether it is the Taos Indians we opt for." McCutchan argues – correctly – that Jackson's inclination was to side with the Pueblo but he wasn't about to be unfaithful to his Senate mentor.

"Scoop was loyal to Clint Anderson. His wife, Helen, was Anderson's secretary when they got married. He truly respected the old man, and liked him," Van Ness recalled. When Anderson asked him for help, Jackson would be there. "And Blue Lake was one of those issues and it wasn't a particularly comfortable place for Scoop to be in. But his friend, Clint Anderson, wanted help, and Scoop went along with that rather than turn on him."

Oklahoma Democrat Fred Harris led the Pueblo cause in the Senate. It was a violation of unwritten Senate rules because this Oklahoma senator was telling a New Mexico senator how to solve a problem in his own state; and, more important, Harris was attempting to outmaneuver both the Indian affairs subcommittee and the full Interior committee. Fred Harris' wife,

John Ehrlichman was almost the deputy president when it came to Indian affairs. He said treaties fit with Nixon's ideas about international law and since American Indians were such a small group of citizens there was a chance government could be successful in improving their lives.

LaDonna, wrote in her memoir, "A Comanche Life," that getting it out of "Anderson's Interior Committee was the hardest. Anderson approached Fred on the floor and said, 'By God, Fred, I don't mess with your Indians in Oklahoma and you shouldn't mess with mine in New Mexico.' Fred just said, "Well, senator, they're not your Indians.' "

The Nixon White House had concerns beyond the Senate. "Nixon faced a difficult decision. His professional staffers were telling him to forget about that 'damn lake in New Mexico' and concentrate on real world issues like ABM," wrote Gordon-McCutchan. He quoted White House aide Bobbie Greene summing up the situation: "Ehrlichman was spending his time and energy again on something that nobody would care about and that Richard Nixon was never going to get any good publicity

President Nixon meets with the leaders of Taos Pueblo on July 8, 1970. The president affirmed his support for the return of Blue Lake on July 8, 1970 — the same day he announced his self-determination policy.

because nobody liked him and the press were never going to give him a fair shake on this."

On Wednesday, July 8, 1970, the White House sided with the Taos Pueblo. President Nixon sent a message to Congress that said the best way to repair the relationship between the United States and Native Americans was to respond "to just grievances which are especially important to the Indian people."

At a press conference with nine Taos elders, the president of the National Congress of American Indians and Vice President Spiro Agnew, Nixon said the record was clear that their land had been taken "without compensation."

"For 64 years, the Taos Pueblo have been trying to regain possession of this sacred lake and watershed area in order to preserve its natural condition and limit its non-Indian use," the president said. "The restoration of Blue Lake lands to the Taos Pueblo Indians is an issue of unique and critical importance to Indians throughout the country. I therefore take this opportunity to endorse legislation which would restore 48,000 acres of sacred land to the Taos Pueblo people."

The same message included the broader repudiation of termination. "This policy of forced termination is wrong, in my judgment," the president said. "We are proposing to break sharply with the past approaches to Indian problems," the presidential message said. "We suggest a new and coherent policy ... most importantly, we have turned from the question of whether the Federal government has a responsibility to Indians to the question of how that responsibility can best be furthered."

What was Nixon's motivation for the sharp break with the past? Ehrlichman said there were three reasons. First, the Constitution was clear that treaties were the supreme law of the land. This fit with Nixon's ideas about international law. Second, American Indians were such a small group of citizens, there was a chance that the government could do something successful to improve their lives. Third, and Ehrlichman said this was Nixon's favorite reason, it was a thank you to Whittier College football coach Wallace J. "Chief" Newman. "I think I admired him more and learned more from him than any man I have ever known aside from my father. Newman was an American Indian, and tremendously proud of his heritage," Nixon wrote in his memoirs. "There is no way I can adequately describe Chief Newman's influence on me. He drilled into me a competitive spirit and the determination to come back after you have been knocked down or after you lose."

There's one more reason. John Ehrlichman was almost a deputy president. On issues involving Indian affairs – including Blue Lake – Nixon was given a briefing after key decisions had already been made. Nixon simply concurred. Nonetheless, Nixon's message set the standard of "self-determination without termination."

But on Capitol Hill that sharp break from the past forced members to redefine their views on American Indian issues. Here was a Republican president – Eisenhower's vice president during the termination era – supporting both self-determination and the return of Indian land. The White House was listening to voices of elected tribal leaders, historians and social critics.

But the politics in the Senate were changing, too. The hearings had been so contentious in the past that a headline in The New Mexican once read: "Senators ridicule Taos Indians challenge in Blue Lake struggle." But by 1970, Anderson was visibly ill. "He could hardly speak at public hearings," Van Ness recalled. When witnesses couldn't understand Anderson, Van Ness said he often translated, but even then the questions were on point and you knew that "the old man" knew what he was talking about.

Anderson's strategy was to keep the House version of the bill, H.R. 471, bottled up in committee – a plan that had worked in the previous two sessions. Anderson told Harris bluntly that if he didn't accept the compromise, no bill would move out of the committee. However, Harris promised to attach the House bill as a rider to every piece of legislation moving out of the Interior Committee so the full Senate could debate it. Anderson responded with a last-minute compromise allowing both measures to move out of the committee and forward for debate.

Nixon told Ehrlichman that if the White House was going to take on Chairman Jackson, then they had better win. Ehrlichman described the situation in the Senate: A Republican president was working with a coalition of liberal Democrats – Fred Harris, Ted Kennedy and George McGovern – to pass the bill over the objection of other Democrats. Ehrlichman said he even acted as a "whip" on the floor of the Senate making phone calls, counting votes and applying pressure.

Barry Goldwater, the Republican from Arizona, was the champion from the right. He told his colleagues that he understood the sacredness of Indian land "just as we have the right to go to a church of our choice."

Jackson once again made the case against the transfer of land as a dangerous precedent and Anderson delivered a powerful defense of the concept of the Forest Service itself. Jackson remained loyal to Clint Anderson. He wasn't about to rebuff his close friend and mentor – even if his own views about Indian issues were evolving.

On Dec. 2, 1970, the Senate voted down the Interior Committee substitute, 56 to 21. Then the Senate voted 70 to 12 to return Blue Lake to its original owners.

Time magazine praised President Nixon for "keeping his pledge, made last July, to open a 'new era in which Indian future is determined by Indian acts and Indian decisions.' The measure never would have gotten to the Senate floor without presidential pressure on members …"

Jackson remained one of the dozen who voted no.

CHAPTER FOUR

Hiring Forrest Gerard, the First Step Forward

Senator Henry M. Jackson had been the guest of honor at a ceremony in Toppenish, Wash., in February 1970. The senator was being formally adopted into the Yakama Indian Nation. "He was given a feather headdress and the Indian name, Eagle-who-protects-the-land," reported the NCAI Bulletin. Representatives from tribes across the region joined in, the Spokanes, Lummis, Makahs, Colvilles, Alaska Natives – as well as emissaries from Taos Pueblo.

Taos Gov. Quirino Romero presented Jackson with a bow-and-arrow. Jackson, wearing the feather headdress of a chief, took an arrow from the quiver, placed it in the bow, pulled the string back and posed for pictures. "This arrow is not a symbol of killing," Romero told Jackson. "But rather a symbol of the truth in doing as much as you can for the Indian people." Romero and Taos tribal secretary Paul Bernal asked for Jackson's support in returning the sacred Blue Lake to the Pueblo.

Yakama Chairman Bob Jim added now that Jackson is a "member of the tribe, he won't be able to say, 'your problems with the government.' He'll have to say, 'our problems with the government.'"

Jackson responded: "It is appropriate on Washington's birthday that we pause to remember the real founders of this country who happen to be your people and your ancestors. Despite the fact that we will soon, in 1976, celebrate the 200th anniversary of our country, we still have some distance to go to resolve these outstanding claims, and a long, long way to go in resolving some of the long-term commitments … to make it possible for 'our' people to receive justice."

Just a few weeks before his adoption ceremony, Jackson appeared at the annual convention of the National Congress of American Indians. It was his first visit to the conference in "many years" and the setting was tense. "Many tribes have worried about Jackson's role in pushing termination legislation for the Colville Tribe," said the NCAI Bulletin. "Others are critical of his protection of Indian Affairs Clerk Jim Gamble, who prepares all legislation on Indians for the Senate and who is seen by many as the 'Indians' greatest enemy in Washington.'"

But the meeting went so well that Jackson told the NCAI that they ought to meet more often. He suggested the Senate Committee take a day and spend it with tribal leaders once a year, something that was done with other interest groups. "Delegates applauded this suggestion and hoped that it signaled a new interest in the desires of Indian tribal leaders by the powerful senator from Washington," the NCAI Bulletin reported.

Jackson had a new interest in Indian affairs despite his opposition to the return of Blue Lake (which would have required him to openly snub his mentor and colleague, Sen. Clinton Anderson from New Mexico).

Meanwhile, Jimmy Hovis, the attorney for the Yakama Nation, had been sounding out Forrest Gerard, an impressively qualifed member of the Blackfeet Tribe, about going to work for Jackson. Gerard remembers meeting with Hovis and a few of the senator's other supporters. Jackson was considering a run for president. "They were all up-front about it," Gerard said. "Jackson was told by his political advisers, that if he was serious about seeking the nomination, he had to refurbish his image, particularly on Indian affairs because of his strong support of termination."

Forrest Joseph Gerard had grown up on Montana's Blackfeet Reservation, the son of Fred Gerard Sr. and Rose Douglas Gerard. He was one of eight children – five sons and three daughters – in a family that was centered on ranching.

Gerard's grandfather, Frederick Gerard, was a colorful figure who had traveled from Fort Berthold (leaving behind a family of three Arikara sisters) to trade furs and supplies with the Blackfeet and their Canadian cousins. A family story says one supply train was robbed, resulting in the loss of "goods consisting of mostly liquid items." The so-called supplies must have been booze. Forrest's grandmother was a Blackfeet woman, Katy Rider, and they lived at Fort Benton where his father, Fred, was born in 1872.

Fred Gerard had an aptitude for cattle ranching. He worked in the Fort Benton area until he was hired by the Bureau of Indian Affairs in 1898, essentially to manage tribal herds on the recently reduced Blackfeet Reservation. He later met and married Rose Douglas, also a mixed-blood Blackfeet, whose family ranched near Augusta, Mont. By 1913 Gerard had left the government and was ranching on family-allotted land near the Middlefork of the Milk River on the reservation.

"The childhood I had there would have been the envy of any young boy in the United States," Forrest Gerard said. "We had a horse of our own. We could walk maybe 15 or 20 yards have some of the best trout fishing in northern Montana. We had loving parents. We had love, support and discipline. And this was my universe, this was a world I knew."

That world changed in 1932, when, for financial reasons, his family moved into the town of Browning. To survive during the Great Depression, his father ran for a seat as a County Commissioner, winning two six-year terms.

At first Forrest Gerard was devastated because it was the end of his idyllic rural life. "The thing I didn't realize as a youngster back then was – love, support and discipline were merely moving from one geographic location to another. Those same attributes of a family were moving with us." He says it was a lesson that stuck with him throughout his career.

And like many children on the reservation during that era, Forrest's parents decided he would be better off speaking English instead of Blackfeet. His father, who was fluent in both languages, believed this was the only route to success in the white man's world.

Gerard was ready to leave high school early, after Pearl Harbor was bombed. "But my father said the war would still be around when I got my diploma," he said. A few months later, "I got my diploma on one hand and on the other got a message, 'Greetings from the United States, you have been inducted.'"

The military was a new world for the young man from Browning. He entered into a highly disciplined structure. He also found himself in a diverse group of men from across the United States. Gerard was assigned to fly on B-24 bomber missions with the 15th Air Force based in southern Italy. "I was only 19 when I flew the first bombing mission in September of 1944. We were forced to face life and death, bravery and fear at a relatively young age. That instilled a little bit of maturity into us that we might not under normal circumstances," Gerard said.

Forrest Gerard

Gerard ultimately served as an engineer and gunner with the 456 Bomber Group, and flew 35 combat missions over Nazi-occupied Europe. Gerard was the natural leader of the enlisted men, despite his age (several were significantly older). The maturity gained through his war experience helped him prepare for life's challenges. There was another bonus: the GI Bill of Rights and the opportunity for veterans to attend college. Gerard was the first member of his family to do so and the first to graduate from what is now the University of Montana. "Looking back," he said, "it was more than just getting an education, it gave me mobility."

His first job after college was with the Montana State Department of Public Instruction. His career took him to Wyoming and then on to Washington, D.C., where in 1957 he was hired by the newly created Indian Health Service as the tribal affairs officer. In that post, Gerard created a wide network of personal contacts ranging from congressional staff to tribal leaders.

Another major step was taken in 1966 when Gerard was selected for a coveted Congressional Fellowship.

Ben Reifel, a Lakota and former Bureau of Indian Affairs area director, had been elected to Congress as a Republican from South Dakota. There had been a handful of American Indians serving in that body, dating back to the early part of the

20th century. But very few – probably only one or two – American Indians had ever worked with the Congress as professional staff members. And no one from Indian Country had worked directly on Indian issues. Gerard's first thought was to use the fellowship to join Reifel's staff. "I went and visited his chief of staff," Gerard said, "and they were gracious, and all that, but I don't think Ben ever hired an Indian."

Reifel was probably trying to redeem himself with the Republicans. "You know, Ben was an outcast in the Republican Party after he voted for that (1968 Indian) civil rights bill," Gerard said. "When Nixon was elected president, old Karl Mundt, ranking minority on the (Senate) Appropriations Committee, arranged for Nixon to visit South Dakota and he just totally shut him out."

Instead, Gerard worked for Democrats Rep. Al Ullman from Oregon and then for South Dakota Sen. George McGovern. "I did extensive legislative research on the Food for Freedom Bill, which was pending before the Senate Committee on Agriculture," Gerard wrote. He also drafted a major policy speech for McGovern, outlining a new policy approach to Indian affairs in early 1966. "The foremost characteristic of our Indian policy should be self-determination for the people it serves," McGovern said. "Too often in the past the federal government has done what it has thought best for Indians, with minor regard for the hopes and aspirations of the Indians." In addition to self-determination, McGovern said a new policy ought to focus on self-help, be consistent, have enough resources to be successful and allow for innovation. The Senate passed McGovern's resolution, but it failed in the House.

Gerard was offered a job with the Public Health Service's Office of Congressional Affairs after his fellowship, a post that would have taken him out of the Indian field. But about that same time, Bob Bennett, who was then Commissioner of Indian Affairs, told Gerard that it was one thing to be critical of the BIA, but it was another to work within the agency to improve services for Indian people. It was a put-up or shut-up moment. Bennett hired Gerard as the BIA's Director of Legislation and Congressional affairs in 1966.

"I jumped at the opportunity and never regretted it because it enhanced my knowledge on how policy and legislation emerge in government and the impact on Indian people," he said.

A year later, John Gardner, the Secretary of Health, Education and Welfare, was heading up a White House plan to transfer all of the Indian affairs functions to his department. A story about the idea was mentioned at a House Interior Committee meeting and was reported in The New York Times on Feb. 11, 1967. Word spread quickly across Indian Country because it represented a possible government shift in policy without any dialogue with tribal leaders.

Six days later, Gardner hastily met with tribal leaders in Kansas City. As Vine Deloria Jr. wrote in, "Custer Died For Your Sins," the chairmen asked for assurances that treaty rights would be protected if the BIA moved to HEW. Absolutely. Of course. Then one Indian leader cut to the chase: "Why ... if there are to be no changes at all, do you want to transfer the bureau to HEW? It would be the same as now. It suddenly occurred to everyone that the chairmen had successfully trapped Gardner in a neat box from which there was no escape. Suffice it to say, there was no transfer."

However, Gardner still pursued a broader program for American Indians at HEW, especially helping those who lived in urban areas and did not receive services from the BIA. A new

Sen. Henry M. Jackson hired Forrest Gerard in 1971 for the Senate's Committee on Interior and Insular Affairs as the professional staff member working on Indian affairs.

Office of Indian Progress was created and in 1967 Gerard was recruited as its director. This meant creating an identity for the agency – and for American Indians – within the massive department. Two specific ideas that took root were the creation of an Indian data bank to provide better statistics and a National Indian Training Institute. The office was also tasked with researching and preparing material for a presidential statement on Indian policy.

The latter had its result, so that on March 6, 1968, President Lyndon B. Johnson sent a message to Congress about the Forgotten American. "The American Indian, once proud and free, is torn now between white and tribal values; between the politics and the language of the white man and his own historic culture. His problems, sharpened by years of defeat and exploitation, neglect and inadequate effort, will take many years to overcome," the president said. "But recent landmark laws – the Economic Opportunity Act, the Elementary and Secondary Education Act, the Manpower Development and Training Act

– have given us an opportunity to deal with the persistent problems of the American Indian."

Johnson proposed a new goal for Indian programs, one that called for a standard of living equal to America as a whole. "A goal that ends the old debate about 'termination' of Indian programs and stresses self-determination; a goal that erases old attitudes of paternalism and promotes partnership self-help," he said. But the president's words fell flat. Neither the Congress nor the country was yet ready for such substantive change. Perhaps it was because of the president's morass in Vietnam or because of the coming 1968 election.

But by 1971, the Senate's Henry Jackson was ready for a new direction – and hiring Forrest Gerard was the first step forward.

During a series of interviews, Gerard was clear about his limits. He remembered saying he wouldn't want to join the committee "to be a brown face on the staff if Jackson was going to pursue the same policies. You don't need me for that."

One reason Gerard was so ideally situated for Jackson's staff was his talent for discovering practical solutions to thorny political problems. He could work with Jackson and chart a path for American Indians that would win support in Congress.

Gerard was hired in February and replaced the "greatest enemy" of Indian Country, Jim Gamble. The official word was that Gamble would spend his time mostly on issues related to the U.S. Territories because of "an ever-increasing" amount of legislation. "These increased responsibilities are within the jurisdiction of the Subcommittee on Territories and, in the future, will require Mr. Gamble's full-time and attention," Jackson said in a press release. "The committee is fortunate in obtaining Mr. Gerard's services to assist in developing new policies and legislative measures designed to serve the needs and interests of the Nation's Indian people. He will, I believe, be in a unique position to work with the committee in the development of innovative and responsive federal programs."

Jackson wasn't interested in a symbolic hiring anymore than Gerard was willing to be a brown face on bad public policy. Both wanted action. Gerard's background and temperament fit with that idea because he already had the experience and a strong network of relationships with tribal leaders and government officials. He had earned respect as a steady, professional leader.

From the very beginning, Jackson said Gerard's appointment was setting the stage for the Interior Committee to launch a far-reaching review of American Indian policy.

He wasn't tossing out political hyperbole. But it's one thing when a senator changes his mind. It's quite another thing when that senator is chairman of a full committee. It means the agenda changes – and it means an unexpected surprise for the Western state senators serving on the Interior and Insular Affairs Committee.

Idaho's Sen. Frank Church was particularly troubled by the policy shift. He was one of a declining number of Democrats who supported termination even after the Kennedy and Johnson administrations had abandoned that cause. Frustrated by that shift, plus the failure of his own initiative to reform the process for dividing Indian lands among heirs, Church resigned his chairmanship of the Indian Affairs subcommittee in 1964. But he was still a member of the full Interior Committee and was blindsided by Gerard's appointment by Chairman Jackson.

The very night Gerard was hired, he bumped into Church at

a Capitol Hill art show. At the event, he was introduced to the senator as the committee's new staff person on Indian affairs. The senator was taken aback. "Why wasn't I notified about this earlier?"

"I don't know, senator," Gerard recalls responding. "I am just a new employee." But he remembers thinking, "Go ask Jackson."

Consider the situation: On one hand, Henry Jackson as the Interior Committee Chairman – a senator not totally trusted by Indian Country – ready to review and reverse federal policy. On the other hand, a group of powerful senators – including those who served on the Interior Committee – continued to advocate for the steady termination of federal services, programs and recognition of tribal governments.

"There was no room for a major error," Gerard recalled. There had to be a careful balance that protected Jackson's leadership in order to move constructive Indian policy legislation forward. One building block present was a lot of new thinking on the Interior Committee, especially the chief counsel, Bill Van Ness.

"Bill was a breath of fresh air and some on the committee weren't too happy to see their position on termination quite literally cut out from under them by the chairman of the committee," Gerard said, "including Sen. Frank Church."

But Jackson trusted Gerard and Van Ness. So when the two agreed on a course, that was most often the direction pursued.

"I wanted some move to send a signal to the field that Jackson was indeed really going the other way," Gerard said. "I reasoned that since termination could trace its origins to a congressional act, House Concurrent Resolution 108, why not have a Senate Concurrent Resolution against termination?"

Van Ness liked the idea. The draft was put together and the

resolution introduced. The American Indian Press Association called Senate Concurrent Resolution 26 "a significant step toward reversing the federal policy of termination." The resolution defined a sense of Congress as a "government-wide commitment to enable Indians to determine their own future, protection of Indian property and identity, raising the social and economic level of Indians, and assistance for urban Indians."

Gerard said Bob Jim, a tribal leader from Yakama, was meeting with committee staff not long after the resolution was introduced. He was excited when he heard about it and immediately took the resolution to the National Tribal Chairman's Association meeting in D.C. Once there, Jim proclaimed that Jackson had turned against termination. The resolution served its purpose; it was a signal to Indian Country that there was a new ally on Capitol Hill.

Jackson spoke for the resolution on the Senate floor. He said termination had a "disastrous impact on the administration of Indian affairs." The resolution passed on Dec. 11, 1971.

The senator from Washington was making good on the promises he made back home to the Yakama Nation. Jackson said it was just the beginning of a "long, long way to go in resolving some of the long-term commitments" made to American Indians.

CHAPTER FIVE

And Now We Move Into Alaska

There is a special relationship between Washington state and Alaska. Seattle is a hub for commerce, tourism and politics. In many ways senators from Washington have always considered Alaska as a permanent constituency. But this relationship was even stronger for Henry M. Jackson because, as chairman of the Interior and Insular Affairs committee, his committee was clearly responsible for writing the federal laws to chart the course for the new state. This was a particularly complicated notion when it involved the first Alaskans.

Americans somehow lump all history involving the people native to this country into one easy-to-digest meal. It's as if there is no difference between Plains Tribes in the Dakotas and Pueblo villages in New Mexico. The American political and legal system attacked the so-called civilized tribes of the Southeast with as much rancor as it did the tribes still in a state of war in Arizona. Indians are Indians. Yet there has been one long exception to the notion of the Indian as a singular entity and that is Alaska Natives.

Alaska Natives, like the native people of the interior United States, have a history dating back thousands of years. But what's different is that Russia – not Britain, Spain or France – was the "great power" that transferred title to the United States in the Treaty of Cession of 1867. That document was supposed to protect the "liberty, property, and religion" of the Russian subjects who remained under the jurisdiction of the United States. That treaty also suggested the Alaska Natives, identified as "uncivilized tribes," would become "subject to such laws and regulations as the United States may, from time to time, adopt in regard to the aboriginal tribes of that country."

Mostly, Congress ignored Alaska Native issues, although the 1891 Homestead Act – allowing settlers claim to 160 acres – expressly exempted lands "to which the Natives of Alaska have prior rights by virtue of actual occupation."

In 1934 when Congress passed the Indian Reorganization Act, creating a structure for government-to-government relations between tribes and the United States, there wasn't any thought given to how that would impact native villages in Alaska.

Flathead anthropologist D'Arcy McNickle reviewed the implementation of the IRA for the government in 1936. "We have made only a beginning. The growing season for any organic law is slow in starting and long in maturing," he wrote. "And now we move into Alaska."

And now we move into Alaska.

The BIA considered Alaska a special case – one all but ignored – that was a challenge as immense as the state itself. Alaska Natives do not fall into "well-defined tribal groups," he wrote, having "traditions of tribal organization and a background of government recognition … and even the status of land ownership is an ambiguous one, which in some cases will have to be clarified before organization work can be proceed."

McNickle's apprehension was partly because the BIA had less experience with Alaska and its unique history. Most Alaska

Natives did not live on reservations, but in villages spread across the state, most maintaining a subsistence lifestyle that had changed little in generations. The BIA did operate schools and provided limited medical services, but largely ignored the issues of governance. The Indian Reorganization Act did not even include Alaska Natives until it was amended in May 1936.

Alaska Federation of Natives leader and state Sen. Willie Iggiagruk Hensley recalls learning about American Indians when he attended college in Washington, D.C. "The more I learned, the more questions I had," he wrote in his memoir, "Fifty Miles from Tomorrow." "Why was there a Bureau of Indian Affairs, but not Bureau of Inuit Affairs? Why did the Indians have reservations, while Alaska had ... more than two hundred Native villages? It may sound naïve, but I struggled to make sense of American history: How could these European guys come over and plant a flag and colonize the land in the name of the king or the queen or the tsar when there were all these people here already?"

Alaska's 1959 statehood essentially postponed the debate until a later time. Questions about native rights to land ownership (and land losses) as well as the inherent powers of governance were ignored. But in 1968 the discovery of North Slope oil was a dramatic development that demanded a settlement of land claims – and title certainty.

"This is a problem Congress agreed to resolve at least a century ago," Hensley told a gathering at the Smithsonian's Folk Life Festival after the discovery. He drew laughs when he warned, "The land issue should be resolved first in Alaska before we give you more gas to run your cars all around the country."

Congress, the Senate Interior Committee and its chairman, Henry M. Jackson, were eager for a resolution to the land

Chairman Jackson and Interior Committee Chief Counsel William Van Ness.

claims. Jackson assigned William Van Ness the task of writing the legislation to make it so. The issue should have been fixed at statehood, but it was put off because the subject matter was complex and few knew enough about Alaska Native issues. "One of the frustrations I had was the Department of the Interior and the Library of Congress, they didn't know anything about the subject matter either. Virtually, absolutely nothing," Van Ness recalled. "How many people were there? Where did they live? What was their socioeconomic condition? What was their education level? Their health, what services were provided? What were their needs? What was the legal case for a settlement?"

Van Ness told Scoop there could not be any legislation until these questions were answered. He suggested hiring a consulting firm "to fill in some of the blanks." But after discussions with other senators, Scoop opted to turn the task over to the Federal Field Committee for Development Planning in Alaska. This panel was appointed by President Johnson to come up with ideas for rebuilding Alaska after the 1964 Anchorage earthquake. Joe FitzGerald, the Field Committee's chairman, was an aviation attorney but, more important, was also a friend of the president.

The committee produced "Alaska Natives & The Land" in October 1968, six months after given the assignment, as a comprehensive look at Alaska Natives that became a framework for the settlement discussion.

"Alaska Native land claims, coming at a time of major resource discoveries and as the state is entering a period of rapid economic development, present a problem, which, in scope and urgency, is the most important problem facing the state today," the report said. "A problem, which can only be resolved at the national level."

The Field Committee said any settlement should include three major elements: The recognition and protection of land and land rights for Alaska Native villages, including the land used for subsistence hunting and fishing; Compensation (either in land or money) for lands taken in the past or as a result of the settlement; and, finally, the establishment of organizations for the management and administration of future revenues.

The Field Committee helped frame the debate for the government.

And the 1962 birth of the Tundra Times added the voice of Alaska Natives to the settlement process. "It will be a medium to air the views of native organizations. It will reflect their policies as they work for the betterment of native people of Alaska," founding editor Howard Rock wrote in his first editorial. "It will reflect their aims … will strive to aid them in their struggle for self-determination and in the settlement of their enormous problems."

Rock, an Eskimo, published from Fairbanks a statewide, twice-monthly publication that set out to create a political alliance with all of Alaska native communities. "Initially, the newspaper was to focus on Alaskan Eskimo concerns, and it was to be named the Inupiat Okatut or Eskimos Speak. However, quite rapidly it became evident that Alaskan Natives were facing broad common concerns," wrote Tamara Lincoln and David Hales in an academic paper, "The Tundra Times: Voice of the Alaskan Natives – Past and Future Perspectives." Perhaps this philosophy is symbolically best represented by the manner in which the Tundra Times addressed its audience. In the upper corner of the front page, the paper's readers were addressed in four languages: Unangauq – "The Aleut's Speak"; Dena Nena Henash – "Our Land Speaks" (Athabascan); Utkah neek – "Informing and Reporting" (Tlingit); and Inupiat Paitot – "People's Heritage" (Eskimo).

Lincoln and Hales concluded that the Tundra Times "played a pivotal role" leading up to the Alaska Native Claims Settlement Act, giving voice to 55,000 native people.

The Tundra Times represented both a broader community voice, and one for the native villages and organizations. But in 1968 the Alaska Federation of Natives became the statewide political coalition that unified Alaska Native groups.

"The younger, more educated Natives who formed the core of AFN leadership sought a settlement that would allow them to keep a portion of their aboriginal lands and quickly learned to organize politically to gain power," wrote Gary C. Anders in

Celebrating the vote for Alaska Statehood in the United States Senate, 1959.

"Social and Economic Consequences of Federal Indian Policy: A Case Study of the Alaskan Natives," "Almost from the beginning, the AFN leadership seemed to insist on corporations as a settlement vehicle. Reasons given for the selection of corporations deal mainly with the Natives' desire to reduce the bureaucratic control of the Bureau of Indian Affairs." No corporation would require the federal's government permission before acting. There would be no "trustee."

"Something very strange happened in the late 1960s. You had a bunch of young men and some women, but mostly men, who were 18 to 23, 24 years old. Only one of whom, as far as I knew, had a college education, and that was Willie Hensley. Some of the others had high school educations, usually from one of the boarding schools in the southeast or the Lower 48 states. A lot of them had grade-school educations or partial grade-school educations, but these people were savvy. They had good judgment. They had great political skills. They were capable of hitting the ground running in Washington, D.C., and dealing with the top lobbyists and lawyers for the oil companies, senators and congressmen, highly trained staff, lawyers and economists. And they held their own," Van Ness recalled.

Indeed, the Alaska Native settlement process was very different from any previous settlement claim. From the beginning it was clear there would be a transfer of land (and money) to native control. In most American Indian claims cases over the years, only money was paid to extinguish title.

Sen. Jackson set a public hearing for Anchorage on Feb. 18, 1968, at the Fourth Avenue Theater. He wanted to hear from the Native community. Some 2,000 people signed up to testify with a strict three-minute rule. "We started at 6 in the morning and ran through until 10:30, 11 o'clock at night," Van Ness said. Sens. Jackson, and Lee Metcalf, and Van Ness, stayed at the Captain Cook Hotel. Because the hearings started so early, they could not get breakfast, only coffee. Cups in hand the three men walked to the hearing. "The first day we walked down Fourth Avenue and walked by restaurants and bars, each with crude, hand-drawn signs that said, "No dogs allowed. No Natives allowed." This infuriated Lee Metcalf, and Scoop was upset with it, so they went in and started tearing these goddamned signs down," Van Ness recalled. "This was my first introduction ... and it said a lot about Alaskan attitudes towards Native people, towards the settlement and that was the way we got started."

Back in Washington, the legislation process had begun. Van Ness relied on the work of the Field Committee – and some of the staff – for a first draft of the legislation. But while Alaska Natives were speaking with a clear, unified voice, other constituent groups were divided. The state of Alaska had changed its positions on a settlement after a gubernatorial election.

The same was true of the state's two senators, Mike Gravel and Ted Stevens. It's hard to imagine two more colorful and conflicting characters representing the same state. Gravel was a candidate in the 2008 Democratic presidential primaries – a quixotic campaign that infuriated many in his party – but hardly collected enough votes to warrant attention. Stevens was the longest-serving Republican U.S. senator in history and had become one of the body's most powerful members, using his seat on the Appropriations Committee to channel federal dollars toward Alaska. But in 2008 (in the middle of an election season), Stevens was indicted by a federal grand jury. He was later vindicated, but lost his Senate re-election by fewer than 4,000 votes.

Stevens and Gravel were hardly on the same page when it came to the land claims.

"These guys had a history. They both served in the Legislature; one was a Democrat and one was a Republican, and they didn't agree when they were in the Legislature together, and they didn't agree on how to go about reaching a settlement on the Native claims issue," Van Ness recalled. "Now, the tradition in the Senate was that if you're a freshman junior member, you sat up at the far end of the table and you didn't speak. You were there to listen and hear what the seniors had to say. Well, they got it backwards. And so they spent a good part of the executive session arguing with each other in louder and louder voices. The chairman finally banged his gavel and put them in their places. He told them that was to be the end of it. Well, when they got up at the end of the meeting they were still yammering at each other, and I walked over and got between them as they went out the door. They both had their dukes up a little bit and the animosity spilled over. They never really got that deal worked out. There was always tension and rivalry and disagreement. It was interesting to watch, and in some respects it was useful, because they were competitive. In terms of ideas, concepts and working for their constituents, some good came out of it."

But while Gravel and Stevens had different approaches, there were relatively few obstacles in Congress. "In terms of politics it wasn't seen as a political issue; it was a difficult problem," Van Ness said. The primary objection from most Republicans and some Democrats was the idea that giving "five, ten, twenty, forty million acres of land to 53,000 people in Alaska plus hundreds of millions of dollars was just crazy. It was outrageous." One particular concern was that American Indians would complain that the claims process in the Lower 48 never included the return of land.

Chairman Jackson had his own ideas about a resolution, partly because of his experience with the Indian Claims Commission. Many Interior Committee members were frustrated by that system because it involved "substantial" claim judgments that were distributed on a per-capita basis. "On many reservations, after a few months, the money was gone and nothing had changed. Nothing good had been done in terms of education or economic development. It just got frittered away by people who had no expectation of managing that kind of money," Van Ness said. "There was great unhappiness with that approach."

There was also no interest in recreating the Indian reservation system by those on the Interior Committee, much less Alaska Native leaders. "So there was an environment where people were quite willing to look at other alternatives," Van Ness said. The Alaska Native leaders "wanted their, they wanted their money and they wanted an environment where they could make mistakes and ... be in charge. They did not want any trusteeship."

In a commentary for the American Indian Press Association, Thomas Edwards dismissed the settlement proposals as "a repetition of history." He wrote: "Out of the hearings came a business as usual attitude – that the government can be relied upon to remain consistent with the last 195 years of its dealings with Native Americans. The whole mess adds up to a monumental land grab ... (because members of Congress are under pressure) from oil, gas and timber interests to get them off their congressional duffs and motivate their cash register ethics into action – a move which should have been taken 104 years ago or at least before the 1959 Alaska Statehood Act."

Edwards compared the settlement proposal to the termination of Wisconsin's Menominee Tribe. "Let's turn it around and look at the real situation. The Natives are being forced to give up their land under the traditional principle of manifest destiny and all they're asking for is a fair shake," Edwards wrote. "The clincher in all of this gumbo is blanket termination."

Van Ness said in a way the Alaska Native Claims Settlement Act was a termination bill. "But on the other hand, it was what the native leadership wanted, so there was no hay to be made by calling it a termination bill," Van Ness said. "We made an effort in the bill to deflect the termination question because those of us working on the bill wanted all of the BIA health and social welfare programs to continue and to be available to Alaska Natives. Ted Stevens, in the end, came around to that point of view and became very effective in the appropriations committee maintaining and preserving those programs."

That was the distinction that made the Alaska Native Claims Settlement Act different from termination. The major flaw of the termination bills of the 1950s and 1960s was the failure of Congress actually to come up with their share of the deal, either in money or land. Termination was forced on tribes and the financial incentives disappeared. But in Alaska, Stevens found the money so that the Natives weren't left impoverished by the transaction.

Under the original statehood legislation, the state of Alaska claimed 103 million acres from the 375 million acres available. The negotiations then boiled down to how much land and money would Alaska Natives accept for their title (allowing the oil companies legal access).

The Nixon administration recommended that Alaska Natives secure title to at least 40 million acres, while the Alaska Federation of Natives sought an additional 20 million acres. But Nixon was clear on one thing: It would be a negotiated settlement. The president promised to veto any measure that was not supported by AFN.

By the summer of 1971, congressional support was in doubt even with the White House backing. Many Republicans in the Senate, including Arizona's Barry Goldwater and Paul Fannin, were against the bill.

On the House side, The Tundra Times reported on last-minute negotiations between Interior and Insular Affairs Chairman Wayne Aspinall, Democrat from Colorado, and the Alaska Federation of Natives that displayed a new "willingness to compromise on many of the major issues of the claims question." But even that deal showed the fragile nature because Aspinall promised to spike the legislation if a more generous bill emerged from the Senate.

The Senate passed its version Nov. 1. Jackson called the bill "the product of four years of hearings and countless executive sessions which were dedicated to the preparation and drafting of a settlement package which provides legal justice to all of the parties involved – the Native people, the state of Alaska, and the federal government." The bill pledged some billion dollars in appropriations and royalties – money that would be spent by 12 new entities, Native corporations. The land selection was to be village-by-village and prior to any state selection of lands.

"Alaskans and Indians numbering nearly 100 were in the Senate gallery as the final vote was taken, and Alaskans later held a celebration in a hotel on Capitol Hill," the American Indian Press Association reported.

The White House – after checking with AFN – signed the settlement into law on Dec. 18. "It is a milestone in Alaska history, and in the way our government deals with Native and Indian peoples," President Nixon said.

It was one of the largest real estate deals in history. Nixon's signature shifted ownership of more than 148 million acres – a landmass larger than all of New England – to the state of Alaska. Native villages and corporations secured title to 44 million acres and $963 million. Tom Richards Jr., writing in The Tundra Times, called it "the last major land treaty between the U.S. government and the aboriginal inhabitants of this country."

The key to effecting that treaty was the careful balancing of competing interests: the Alaska Federation of Natives, the state's officials and congressional delegation, the Nixon administration and powerful members of Congress. At the same time, the boundaries of those competing interests were evolving. There were an increasing number of American Indian and Alaskan professionals working in government agencies and there was a growing sophistication of tribal leaders who made their cases directly to the Congress.

CHAPTER SIX

Making Self-Determination the Law of the Land

Forrest Gerard was, as he put it, a new employee at the Senate Interior and Insular Affairs Committee in early 1971. In the short history of the United States there may have been other American Indians working on Capitol Hill, but none were given Gerard's broad mandate. Consider the dynamic here: Sen. Henry Jackson was reversing himself on an Indian policy – one that he had advocated for many years – and now he was trusting a new employee to chart the next steps forward.

But who in Indian Country would believe Scoop Jackson anyway? How does a senator shift from promoting termination to being one with positions advocated by and for American Indians?

Gerard thought it was important that Jackson send a signal – not proof, not yet – at least an indication that the senator had really changed his position. Jackson introduced a Senate resolution to repeal congressional support for termination, House Concurrent Resolution 108.

"Nearly 18 years have lapsed since Congress approved a termination of federal treaty responsibility toward Indian Nations," wrote Thomas Edwards, an Alaska Native, in a commentary for the American Indian Press Association. "Almost two decades of economic stagnancy because tribes did not know when they would face the auction block, two decades of intertribal conflict – the most recent example being the Colville Tribal Council termination fight. And two decades of mistrust of anything that smacked of progress toward a self-sustaining economy because the esteemed lawmakers would say that 'our' Indians no longer need their benevolent hand."

Even President Nixon's message did not call for an outright repeal of 108, Edwards wrote in July 1971. Nor did any of the legislative proposals sent to Capitol Hill from the White House.

"The lone Senate bill was introduced by Sen. Henry Jackson of Washington last month," Edwards wrote. "The bill has several qualities and one wonders if Jackson, whose attitude toward Natives in his own state is reprehensible at best, penned the bill or was ghost-written."

Still, Edwards said, "It's an admirable turnabout for Jackson."

In so many ways, the whole debate about termination ended on July 8, 1971, on the Colville Indian Reservation when the pro-termination was defeated. Two weeks later, in Washington, D.C., a U.S. Senate hearing practically celebrated the end of the termination era.

"President Nixon, Sen. Jackson, and the great majority of American Indians have criticized the general disaster and failure of termination," said Ada Deer, representing the Menominee Enterprises, the remaining authority from the then-terminated tribe. "To Menominees, the real meaning of the termination period is this: Congress decided unilaterally to end its treaty obligations toward us, and attempted to thrust us, unprepared and uninformed, into a way of life completely unacceptable to us."

Another Menominee, George Kenote, said the resolution

was important so that "Indian communities across the land can again feel safe at home."

The Senate formally adopted Jackson's resolution disavowing termination on Dec. 11, 1971. Congress had thus rejected the policy of termination – and with that step came a new interest – and a competition – from senators eager to show their support for Indian causes. This, in turn, created spheres of influence that differed on style as much as substance. Forrest Gerard worked for Scoop Jackson (and his Interior Committee). La-Donna Harris (about whom more later), the wife of Sen. Fred Harris, favored first Robert Kennedy, and then after his death, Ted Kennedy, as the correct senator to reform Indian policy. Some of this was ideological – Jackson was the centrist, while the Harrises were liberals. This tension played out in a variety of ways.

The Indian Education Subcommittee was the platform used by Bobby Kennedy during his extensive travels across Indian Country as part of his 1968 anti-poverty tour. The tour was practically a campaign vehicle in Kennedy's run for the White House. "As a member of the Cabinet and a member of the Senate, I have seen the inexcusable and ugly deprivation that causes children to starve in Mississippi, black children to riot in Watts, young Indians to commit suicide on their reservations because they've lacked all hope and feel they have no future," Kennedy said. "I have traveled and I have listened to the young people of our nation and felt their anger about the war that they are sent to fight and about the world that they are about to inherit."

A young Ted Kennedy picked up the cause after his brother's June 1968 assassination. He wrote in Look magazine two years later: RFK "saw, as I have seen, the resilience of the Indian way of life, a way of life that has for many generations resisted destruction despite government blunders that almost seem designed to stamp it out."

Ted joined Bobby's widow, Ethel, at a National Congress of American Indians banquet in February 1970. "White settlers took Indian lands in the name of progress and civilization; white industrialists and developers have taken Indian lands and water in the name of commercial and industrial development," he told the delegates. "If the federal government is to construct and deliver a meaningful policy for Native Americans then we can no longer be content with the double standard which permits us to spend billions in support of economic development overseas and at the same time pay only lip service to the needs of the original Americans."

Kennedy had two platforms, a special subcommittee of Judiciary and the Subcommittee on Indian education. The special committee on Administrative Practices and Procedures focused on the "misuse, exploitation and diminution" of tribal natural resources by the federal government. "Despite rhetoric to the contrary, Indians are the objects of a continuing policy of termination brought about through destruction of the resource base upon which their future depends," Kennedy said. Kennedy proposed a "receivership" for Indian lands because the government had botched management so badly. He added that the Interior Department's Reclamation Bureau was "the present day, institutional embodiment of General Custer."

Kennedy was challenging his colleagues in the Senate on the Western-domination of not only Indian relations, but of resource management, particularly water rights. He said the BIA and, by implication, the Senate Interior Committee, hadn't done enough to protect Indian water from being stolen by states, cities and private corporations.

He promised a further investigation. But natural resources were the prerogative of Interior – not Judiciary – and the Kennedy proposals were stopped cold in the Senate.

Still, Kennedy promised to champion the Native American cause and to turn to "the American Indian himself" because self-determination is the best solution. The committee was propelled, in part, by a 1969 report that began under Robert Kennedy that called Indian education a "national tragedy." The younger Kennedy's approach was a bill that would have removed education programs from the Bureau of Indian Affairs. On one hand, this was exactly the successful method for creating the Indian Health Service in 1959. On the other hand, removing the largest source of funds and personnel in the BIA seemed to many as a financial version of termination.

Kennedy's subcommittee, of course, reported to Sen. Claiborne Pell's Education Committee instead of Jackson's Interior Committee. Pell assumed and was assured that this education reform would have broad support from Indian Country.

Gerard, from his vantage point on Jackson's staff, recalled a Kennedy aid bragging: "I have never had an education bill that didn't go through relevant committees that … passed through the Senate."

But Kennedy's notion of self-determination did not include listening to Indian Country and many tribes weren't on board with the legislation. The National Congress of American Indians said the bill wasn't thought through enough and urged regional hearings because this act would affect each tribal group differently. The committee's counsel, Steven Wexler, dismissed the NCAI request, saying that tribes could always avail themselves of written testimony.

BIA Commissioner Louis Bruce was also adamantly opposed.

"The education of Indian children must always be viewed as an important component of a number of inter-related functions performed by the Bureau of Indian Affairs with and for Indian people," he testified. "To place the directorship under another level of bureaucracy – however well intended – could well be viewed by Indian people with great hostility and distrust."

But Kennedy pressed on. "This is not an attempt to destroy the bureau, as some people think," Kennedy's representative William Pensoneau said. "I think the bureau is resilient enough, and it will be given a greater amount of time to concentrate on other areas of Indian affairs such as land, which they're set up to do."

Meanwhile, Gerard drafted an alternative – a Jackson education bill. But both bills died when the Senate recessed. "I was told later that Chairman Pell really blew up at Kennedy, saying, 'You told me everything was wired and I can't push a bill down the throats of the Indian people,'" Gerard said.

But that encounter set the stage for the next Congress when that competition with Kennedy would return. The Kennedy people would promote their education bill, while Jackson sponsored the Indian Self-Determination and Education Reform Act.

Round Two immediately caused concern. Many hoped for either a Jackson or Kennedy bill without the renewed competition.

Even the Bureau of Indian Affairs legislative office tried to get Gerard – and his boss Jackson – to back away. They told him: "We're going to have trouble with that bill."

"Why?" Gerard remembers responding. "We're promoting President Nixon's policy. We're going to make it the law of the land."

CHAPTER SEVEN

Fixing the Mistake of Termination

There was now congressional recognition that termination was a mistake. Sen. Henry Jackson's resolution – Senate Concurrent Resolution 26 – passed the upper house in December of 1971. The measure repudiated termination and "affirmed the unique relationship that exists between American Indians and the federal government." The House, however, never took up the measure. Perhaps because there was no need to do anything else: The original termination resolution – House Concurrent Resolution 108 – did not have the force of law. It was only the sense of the 83rd Congress – and it expired in 1955 at the conclusion of that congressional session.

Nonetheless, as the New York City-based advocacy group, the Association on American Indian Affairs, pointed out that even though Resolution 108 had expired, "for nearly two decades it has created an aura of fear and intimidation in the American Indian communities, and U.S. Bureau of Indian Affairs' actions all too often have confirmed Indian suspicions about the intention of the federal government."

But if termination was a policy mistake, how should the government fix it? The Menominees in Wisconsin had an answer: restoration. It was the idea that Congress could restore their status as a tribal government and with that deliver federal services. Early in 1972, Sen. William Proxmire introduced a bill that would re-establish the tribe's corporate and land status. Sen. Gaylord Nelson and every member of the state's House delegation, all supporting the Menominees, joined Proxmire in this cause. Washington Rep. Lloyd Meeds was chairman of the House Indian Affairs Committee and he had taken up the chore of moving a Menominee bill through that body.

"By then I was carpooling with Bill Van Ness," Gerard said. "I told him that it looked certain that the Menominee bill would pass." Gerard suggested that Jackson sign on and "that ought to erase any doubts where he stands on termination."

Gerard and Van Ness worked up a statement from the senator and arranged to get Jackson on the agenda at an NCAI banquet. Gerard said it was a statement with a lot of platitudes, the usual types of things a politician would say to a constituent group. But at the end of his talk, Jackson pulled a letter from his pocket, and read his own announcement that he was signing on to the Menominee Restoration Act as a cosponsor.

"It brought the House down," Gerard recalled. He was standing in the veranda with Jackson's press secretary, who told him, "You really called that one." Still smarting from their legislative competition, a Kennedy's staffer who was attending the dinner was even more direct. "Pretty shrewd move, Gerard," he told him.

Gerard was also shrewd about the politics ahead for President Nixon's 1972 legislative proposals. One bill, the creation of an assistant secretary of Interior for Indian affairs, had general support from tribes. But the Nixon administration disagreed with the language. Interior Secretary Rogers C.B. Morton said the "statutory job descriptions are not in the interest of the department."

Another Nixon proposal would have authorized expanded contracting authority between the federal government and tribes. Gerard crafted the president's language into Jackson's Indian Self-Determination Act of 1972. He told the American Indian Press Association: "I look upon this bill as an alternative to the administration's Assumption of Control Bill, and admit that it does not go as far as their bill. But it is one with a better chance of being moved through the Senate."

The "Indian" agenda on Capitol Hill was as growing and varied as Indian Country itself. There was the president's program, plus the Kennedy initiative and more ideas from Oklahoma Sen. Fred Harris. Harris had won a special election to the Senate in 1964 and a full term two years later. He and Kennedy were decidedly more liberal on a host of issues and were occasionally willing to defy Senate traditions. In 1972, Harris declined to run again – but South Dakota elected the maverick Rep. Jim Abourezk as the replacement for Karl Mundt. The Democrat "is known to be interested in serving on the Senate Indian subcommittee," the American Indian Press Association reported.

More than that: Abourezk was interested in being the Senate's principal voice on all things Indian. "Although I was born and raised on the Rosebud Sioux Reservation in South Dakota," he said, "I don't pretend to be an expert on Indian problems and I have no intention of dreaming up new legislation without asking Indian people and tribes what they think ought to be done."

Indeed, since it's a post that few in the Senate seek, as soon as Abourezk walked into the chamber as a member, he sought and won election as chairman of the subcommittee on Indian affairs. Abourezk replaced his fellow South Dakotan, George

McGovern, who had earned a spot on the prestigious Foreign Relations Committee. In assuming the post, the newly-minted senator said, "In looking at the history of federal-Indian relations, anyone can see the well-documented and tragically consistent pattern of disorganization, ineffective bureaucracy, exploitation and total misunderstanding on the part of the federal government."

Abourezk promised to use his chairmanship to launch "an overview, and possibly an overhaul, of the present structure, administration and policies regarding Indian affairs."

He hired Sherwin Broadhead – the BIA superintendent from the Colville Reservation – as his principal staff member on Indian issues. Broadhead had supported the anti-termination efforts by Lucy Covington. "It is with mixed emotions that we say good-bye," the Colville Tribal Tribune reported. "On the one hand, we are losing a man who has come as close to being a complete Indian advocate as any man can. His leadership and willingness to do battle with the federal bureaucratic powers, both the Bureau of Indian Affairs and the Department of Interior, has brought more federal and local programs and money to the Colville Reservation." But in Washington working for "Senator Abarasque," the tribal newspaper said, misspelling the senator's name, "Sherwin will apply his talents toward developing legislation that will benefit all Indians, including the Colvilles."

However, Abourezk would have a great deal of competition. This was a period of intense and often frenetic legislative activity.

The Bureau of Indian Affairs was torn apart by turf battles, a division between long-serving bureaucrats and the "new" team of Commissioner Louis Bruce (Oglala Sioux), including Ernie

Stevens (Oneida), Leon Cook (Red Lake Chippewa) and Alexander "Sandy" McNabb (Micmaq). By 1971, the old guard had the upper hand when John Crow, an Oklahoma Cherokee, was named deputy commissioner after a long career in the BIA and BLM. Another career employee, Wilma Victor, who had once been reassigned by Bruce to the Phoenix office, was able to reverse that posting because of her long friendship with Interior Secretary Morton. The American Indian Press Association reported that Victor was so pleased at the appointment of Crow that she personally delivered the news to the NCAI's Washington office.

But what made these bureaucratic maneuvers different is that Leon Cook was able to ask Kennedy for oversight hearings with his Subcommittee on Administrative Practices and Procedures. This committee gave Kennedy wide latitude to examine any federal program – and outside of the traditional territory of the Senate Interior Committee.

It was the fight on Indian education reform that was particularly divisive – between those who agreed with the Kennedy approach as opposed to those who favored Jackson.

"We need to know whether or not Indians actually want any legislation passed at all," Kennedy aide Thomas Susman complained at a conference of Indian educators. "Although Indian society is itself pluralistic, if Indians do want legislation passed, they must first seek some internal compromise, not compromise with the Congress. Public sentiment, not the sensitivity of Congress, is the chief asset of the Indian people. … right now what we need is the majority Indian voice."

Indian Country wasn't keen on being the referee between Kennedy and Jackson. At the Affiliated Tribes of Northwest Indians meeting in Lewiston, Idaho, for example, the tribes voted to oppose both bills. There was also a sense from tribal advocates that there was no need to rush into this dispute: House Interior Chairman Aspinall was unlikely to move any legislation. Indian Affairs Subcommittee Chairman Lloyd Meeds, D-Wash., put it this way: "There is not the present impetus there to take the leadership in reform that should be there."

This meant the skirmish, primarily between Kennedy and Jackson staffs, would continue into the next Congress.

Another dimension in the intense and complicated politics of this era was LaDonna Harris. She arrived on the Washington scene with the election of her husband, Fred, in 1964. But her interests, and her contacts, were wide ranging. "From our earliest days in Washington, LaDonna became a first-rate tour guide for Oklahomans who came to visit, as well as for others from around the country, especially American Indian delegations," Fred Harris wrote in his memoir, "Does People Do It?" But those visits meant Vice President Hubert H. Humphrey would – as Harris put it – "sweep LaDonna and me along with him" for a drink, dinner and long conversations.

LaDonna Harris' access continued during the Nixon years. Brad Patterson, who worked at the White House, said he would often run ideas about Indian issues past her before passing them along to his superiors.

By 1972, her primary vehicle was Americans for Indian Opportunity. The organization was modeled after a group that LaDonna Harris founded, Oklahomans for Indian Opportunity. Even that group was subject to the same divisions that were sweeping through the halls of the BIA, Congress and Indian Country. In July 1972, the AIO board of directors fired its executive director and named Harris, the president, as the acting director. The staff opposed the move, issuing a statement that said: "While Mrs. Harris has proven herself a very charming, outgoing and apparently warm person, we who have done the actual implementation of the programs find her to be largely unaware." The AIO board responded by saying that the previous director, and implicitly the staff, had been overly lavish. It was a one-sided contest. Fred Harris left the Senate in 1972, but LaDonna, despite the internal problems, made AIO her most important political platform from then on. As Gerard put it: "She was here, there, everywhere."

Another element in the atmosphere of the times was the role played by the White House's National Council on Indian Opportunity, an appointed group of tribal leaders that consulted with the vice president's office. NCAI executive director Charles Trimble said the council's purpose was to "manipulate" tribal leaders. "I am led to believe that NCIO is a divisive force in Indian affairs and should be looked into."

Another factor was the growing number of American Indian professionals, including scientists, attorneys and a group of journalists who were working for the American Indian Press Association. Franklin Ducheneaux, a Cheyenne River Sioux, had been the NCAI's primary representative and strategist for legislative matters. Then in April 1973, Ducheneaux was hired as consultant on Indian affairs for the House Interior Committee. And, "having an Indian up there is an opportunity to get moving in some of the neglected areas of Indian legislation and problems," Ducheneaux said.

The old, closed-door traditions of the Interior Committee were changing, too. Chairman Jackson promised that committee sessions would be public – unless there was a good reason for closing them (followed by a public explanation).

That new atmosphere was fresh air for Indian issues. The

Menominee Restoration Act was moved through Congress with rare speed. House Interior Chairman Wayne Aspinall was defeated in the Colorado Democratic primary and was no longer an outright obstacle. In October 1973, the House passed the Menominee Restoration Act with a vote 404 to 3. Subcommittee Chairman Meeds said: "I think it is an overwhelming repudiation of the unwarranted and unworkable policy of termination. The size of the vote indicates that most members of the House have realized this."

The Senate moved swiftly – despite early warnings of a slow process from Jerry Verkler at the Interior Committee. President Nixon signed the act into law on Dec. 22, 1973.

"By restoring the Menominee Indian Tribe to federal trust status, the United States has at last made a clear reversal of a policy which was wrong, the policy of forcibly terminating Indian tribal status," Nixon said. "Restoration is a particularly apt course to adopt in this instance because of two characteristics of the Menominees' situation: First, it can be argued that the Menominees did not willingly enter into termination. Secondly, unlike many of the terminated tribes, the Menominees have remained a remarkably cohesive Indian group with their own government and have maintained a strong attachment to their former reservation land."

But while celebrating the Menominee restoration, Nixon also urged Congress to do more. "The legislative agenda in the area of Indian affairs is still a long one and a significant one. Many of the items on that agenda are recommendations, which I made fully three and one half years ago. I am confident that the Congress will continue to move ahead with these tasks in the same constructive and bipartisan spirit."

The first bill to actually be enacted from President Nixon's

1970 proposals was the Indian Finance Act. "I worked with Abourezk and he felt we'd be smart to do that," Gerard said, because there weren't the same differences over policy and form that were present in both the self-determination and education bills.

The bill the Nixon administration sent to Congress was too narrow in its ambitions and was imprecisely drafted. But Gerard had a trick in mind. In order to gain Republican support, Gerard took the Nixon bill, stripped every word after the enacting clause and amended the entire bill with new language. The title was Nixon's, but the text were now Gerard's words. "Abourezk really liked that," Gerard recalled. "He told his brother (who was visiting), 'Look, isn't this great what we're doing? Goddamn administration can't send a decent bill up, but we're putting one together.'"

When it finally passed, the Indian Finance Act of 1974 opened up new sources of capital for reservation development with a revolving loan fund, loan guarantees and insurance programs.

On April 3, 1974, President Nixon said he took special pleasure signing the legislation into law.

"This bill is the second to be enacted of seven measures which I proposed 4 years ago, when I pledged to follow a new philosophy of self-determination for Indians," the president said. "The first, enacted in 1970, returned the Blue Lake lands to the Taos Pueblo Indians. It continues to be my hope that, with the support and encouragement of the Federal Government, we can create a new era in which the future of Indian people is determined primarily by Indian acts and Indian decisions."

CHAPTER EIGHT

A Tutorial in Indian Health Legislation

The success of the Indian Finance Act set the stage for the next round of Indian legislation. There were continuing disputes about how to proceed on Indian education. Forrest Gerard said it was unclear how much of this division was a competition between the staffs versus real debates among the senators themselves. The American Indian Press Association reported it this way in March of 1974: "A vital piece of Indian legislation continues to hang in the balance as two powerful senators, Henry M. Jackson, D-Wash, and Edward M. Kennedy, D-Mass., and Jackson's maverick Indian Affairs Subcommittee Chairman, Sen. James Abourezk, D-S.D., jockey for position and the support of the Indian people."

That three-way competition divided Indian Country too. "The key Indian groups behind Sen. Jackson and his staffer Forrest Gerard, a Montana Blackfeet, have been the National Congress of American Indians and the National Tribal Chairmen's Association. Supporting Kennedy and his staffer Thomas Susman and attorney Harold M. Gross have been the Americans for Indian Opportunity and the National Indian Education Association ... (and) behind Sen. Abourezk and staffer Sherwin Broadhead and other staff aides has been primarily the United Sioux Tribes of South Dakota," AIPA reported.

"And George McGovern, the great liberal, had a sister who was on the school board in Sisseton, So. Dakota, and his people told me George is unhappy with that bill," Gerard recalled. "His sister was beating the hell out of him because they were going to give the Indian parents control of that Johnson-O'Malley money" (a 1930s program that sent federal money to local school districts for Indian education).

The AIPA predicted that "the walls of Jericho began to cave in on the man who had been named in a poll of Senate staff aides as the 'most powerful man in the Senate,' that is Jackson. Waiting for Jackson on the Senate floor was his old Indian education opponent Sen. Kennedy. In 1972, Jackson had ambushed a Kennedy Indian education bill only minutes from final passage in the Senate."

Indeed, Sussman told the news service that he predicted Jackson's Indian education provisions would "never get out of the Congress."

While the Kennedy team was trying to kill the bill, Abourezk's subcommittee was pursuing a major rewrite – working closely with the Kennedy staff. Kennedy and Abourezk focused their efforts on the Indian education aspects of the bill. "They didn't dare attack self-determination," Gerard said.

But the old-line members of the Senate Interior Committee weren't keen on Kennedy's approach. The senator had used the special investigative committee to look at Indian water rights – an area that was perceived as the exclusive Interior Committee prerogative. So the day the bill came up for consideration, a major snowstorm had hit Washington, D.C. "I couldn't get out of my driveway," Gerard recalled. "But good old Sen. Quinton Burdick from North Dakota. I guess he had a pickup with chains on it or something. He got in, was in the Senate, and they called that bill up. He was from the committee and they passed it."

The Kennedy and Abourezk supporters were furious. They maneuvered to have the bill sent back to committee. "That's when the war erupted," Gerard said. However, Gerard was building a majority coalition around the full Interior Committee, including its Republican members. Gerard was selling the bill as the implementation of Nixon's policy, and working closely with Rick Lavis, who was Arizona Sen. Paul Fannin's Indian affairs adviser.

"Indian self-determination came at the right time," Lavis said. "It gave people choices. It spoke to those Republicans who wanted to reform those programs. It spoke to Democrats who wanted better delivery of services. It spoke to those who said, 'Let the tribes do it.'"

Still, the divisions among the Senate's more liberal members continued. Chuck Trimble at NCAI told Gerard: "Your stature would rise if you'd encourage Jackson to strip education from the bill (in order to enact self-determination provisions). I thanked him, and said, 'no.' I thought we were correct." In the end, the NCAI stuck with the Jackson bill and favored it over the alternatives.

But for Jackson, enough was enough. "It was my understanding that Jackson and Kennedy talked on the floor," Gerard said. "They agreed to peace and staffers were instructed to work out a compromise."

Jackson liked Ted Kennedy. He had, after all, been so close to Jack that he was considered the favorite to be the vice presidential nominee. But Jackson did not appreciate Bobby Kennedy's approach with his special committees. "Bobby was sharp-tongued, very liberal, and Scoop didn't trust him," Van Ness recalled. This dates back to Bobby's work as chief counsel for Sen. Joseph McCarthy and the Permanent Subcommittee on Investigations in 1955. Scoop had been a member of that committee and Jackson was one of the first senators to challenge McCarthy's ethics.

To resolve the dispute between the two staffs, the Indian education "reform" was recast as the Education Assistance Act. "Somebody said there isn't much reform here, so we changed the name of the bill, there's always a play of words in political circles," Gerard said. "That was the compromise." But self-determination was a go, though Richard Nixon was no longer president.

"The Congress is to be congratulated for its passage of this legislation. It will enhance our efforts to implement this policy of Indian self-determination," President Gerald Ford stated when signing the Indian Self-Determination and Education Assistance Act into law. "Title I of this act gives the permanence and stature of law to the objective of my administration of allowing – indeed encouraging – Indian tribes to operate programs serving them under contract to the federal government."

Ford said the education provisions would give Indian communities "a stronger role in approving or disapproving the use of funds for children in public schools. It also provides for better planning in the use of these funds to meet the educational needs of the Indian students." He added "the enactment of this legislation marks a milestone for Indian people. It will enable this administration to work more closely and effectively with the tribes for the betterment of all the Indian people by assisting them in meeting goals they themselves have set."

With major accomplishments in the area of governance and education, the time was also right for a sorely needed reform in the Indian health care arena.

President Nixon had asked Congress for more money for Indian health in his 1970 message to Congress. "This administration is determined that the health status of the first Americans will be improved," the president said, adding an appropriations request for an additional $10 million for health programs. But, he said, "These and other Indian health programs will be most effective if more Indians are involved in running them. Yet, almost unbelievably, we are presently able to identify in this country only 30 physicians and fewer than 400 nurses of Indian descent. To meet this situation, we will expand our efforts to train Indians for health careers."

To implement that kind of training, the president needed legal authority, a new law. As a courtesy, the chairman introduced the White House plan in the following Congress, where it languished.

Meanwhile in Seattle, another health reform effort had begun.

"Abe Bergman, a Seattle pediatrician, was a political activist as well as a doctor (or, as some of his colleagues complained, a doctor as well as a political activist)," wrote Eric Redman, in his book, "The Dance of Legislation," "Besides running the outpatient clinic of the Children's Orthopedic Hospital and teaching at the University of Washington Medical School, Bergman served as an unofficial adviser to Senator (Warren) Magnuson." That's how Bergman came to help the senator successfully promote new child-safety legislation. "Magnuson's successes convinced Bergman, in his words, that 'politicians can save more lives than doctors,'" Redman wrote.

Eric Redman was a recent college graduate working on the senator's staff who was assigned the impossible task of working with Bergman on a bill to establish a National Health Service Corps. "The Dance of Legislation" was a chronicle of his experiences on that one bill – including its several "near-death" experiences. At the end of the 91st Congress, Redman said senior members of the Magnuson team told him there wasn't enough time to move any bill; it would have to wait for the next session. "But this decision failed to take account of Bergman. Far from being dissuaded, Bergman seemed to redouble his efforts, and since he had no formal staff position, his efforts consisted largely of badgering and cajoling me," Redman wrote. "Whenever I tried to reason with him, Bergman had a petulant and inflexible reply: There has to be a way. Silently I cursed doctors in politics … however Bergman was right. There was a way."

Indeed there was a way. Magnuson, his staff and Bergman pursued every option until the National Health Service Corps bill finally became law.

That very success also opened up another legislative avenue for the Seattle physician. Bernie Whitebear, a Colville who was running a Seattle urban Indian clinic, took Bergman on a tour. "He showed me around and, of course, it was a terrible place, physically a dump. And they were struggling. They had volunteer doctors and dentists," Bergman recalled. He asked what sort of help was available from the U.S. Indian Health Service, only to learn that program was only for Indians living on reservations.

One of the legislative tricks that was used to create the National Health Service Corps was to expand existing federal programs. So Bergman wondered about adding an urban mission to the Indian Health Service.

"I talked to Senator Jackson," Bergman recalled. "He said, 'It sounds like a good idea, but go see Forrest. Forrest Gerard.

Go see Forrest and talk to him about it.' It was remarkable. It took Jackson all of one minute to agree in principle, but he wasn't going to get into the details because he knew it was a complicated problem."

When Bergman walked into the Senate office for the meeting, Gerard was there along with Dr. Emery Johnson, the director of the Indian Health Service. "I said, 'Hi, Senator Jackson says we can have some legislation for urban Indians,' and I remember Forrest just smiled and said, 'Yeah, yeah, that's really good, but you know it's a little more complicated than that.' There began my tutorial in Indian affairs and Indian health legislation."

Gerard and Johnson had already been considering legislation for a general upgrade of Indian health programs. "Forrest explained that if you went forward with a plan just to improve urban Indian health, it would fail. But he and Emery had a more comprehensive approach, what became the Indian Health Care Improvement Act."

Jackson conducted hearings through the Senate Permanent Investigations Subcommittee – one that gave him free rein to explore the many facets of the problem. Doctors and nurses testified they were working in "crumbling and ill-equipped facilities and being ordered to turn away sick patients who would be hospitalized elsewhere under present medical standards."

Jackson said that more than half – 29 of 51 – Indian hospitals were in such bad condition that they could not meet standards for certification.

"I believe it leads to only one conclusion: The federal government is responsible for medical malpractice against Indians who suffer and die because the department of Health, Education and Welfare doesn't take Indian health care seriously."

Jackson's Indian Health Care Improvement Act had five major components: first, increased scholarships for students in medical and health-related fields; second, improved funding for health services; third, money to upgrade or build new facilities; fourth, entitled eligible American Indians to receive Medicaid or Social Security services; and, finally, authorized contracts for urban Indian health clinics.

Once again it was Nixon's 1970 message that started the process. The president said the Bureau of Indian Affairs (and by implication, the Indian Health Service) wasn't designed to serve the growing percentages of American Indians and Alaska Natives who lived away from their tribal homelands. The result, the president said, were people "lost in the anonymity of the city, often cut off from family and friends, many urban Indians are slow to establish new community ties. Many drift from neighborhood to neighborhood; many shuttle back and forth between reservations and urban areas. Language and cultural differences compound these problems. As a result, federal, state and local programs which are designed to help such persons often miss this most deprived and least understood segment of the urban poverty population." The logical solution to the "most deprived and least understood segment" of Indian country was to invest in health programs specifically designed for native people living in urban areas.

That's exactly what Gerard had in mind. But he also had another motivation. American Indians moved to cities for a variety of reasons, including those who sought better jobs and opportunity. But one key factor was the termination policy: The federal government had paid for the "relocation" of American Indians from reservations to a number of cities along the West Coast, as well as Chicago, Cleveland and Minneapolis. The logic here was that the federal government had an obligation to do something for American Indians in cities because it promoted that migration.

"We often speak of Indian Country, it's an old legal term," said Gerard. "Well, the Indian Health Care Improvement Act applied Indian Country to urban Indians living in metropolitan centers." Gerard said the law didn't build the Indian health system in cities, but it did create an environment where the clinics could tap into some federal money, plus community funding and grants.

One of the challenges Gerard and his allies faced was making certain that Jackson's Interior and Insular Affairs Committee would have jurisdiction over the bill. There was early support from the Senate Finance Committee (because the law included Medicaid and Medicare provisions) that made it clear they weren't pursuing jurisdiction – and would support the measure (even supplying some of the technical language).

Bergman described the Indian Health Care Improvement Act as an "amazing piece of legislation" because it documented the need and the rationale as part of the law.

Still fresh from the competition with the Kennedy staff, Gerard said an early fear was that the bill would be referred to Kennedy's Health and Labor Committee.

"So we engineered a meeting with the National Indian Health Board. Mel Sampson from Yakama agreed to ask, at the appropriate time, if Sen. Kennedy would forgo jurisdiction so that we might pass a bill," Gerard said. "Amazingly, he agreed to do that at the meeting. I don't think his staff was too happy."

Gerard, however, called it "a godsend."

Jackson also immediately reached across the aisle and sought support from the ranking Republican on the committee, Arizona Sen. Paul Fannin, and Rick Lavis on his staff.

Lavis said he had to sell Fannin – a conservative – on the cost of the legislation, $1.6 billion. "It's costing how much?" Fannin asked. But the facts on the ground overwhelmingly supported the case. "The Indian Health Service was in total disarray – not as an organization – but in terms of facilities, its manpower, its ability to deliver health care." Moreover, Lavis said the facilities in Arizona were deplorable, basically houses connected by walkways and other inadequate facilities. Republicans also came together around the idea that the health care improvement bill satisfied treaty obligations, rather than serving up another big government anti-poverty program.

Bergman said the broad coalition was the key – and the greatest danger to the bill's success came from the liberal members of the Senate who "always wanted more."

The Indian Health Care Improvement Act was what Lavis called a "harmonic convergence." It had broad support from the American Indian community, doctors, church groups and key officials in the Nixon and Ford administrations.

The bill died in the 93rd Congress when the House failed to complete its side of the legislative process. "So we had to do it again," Lavis recalled. Forrest and Lavis went back fully prepared with briefing books and the evidence about why the law was necessary. But someone on the committee interrupted the two men before they started. "Don't you understand," Lavis remembers hearing, "you have the votes. Now, shut up." Fifteen minutes later, the $1.6 billion bill moved through the committee.

The bill that finally passed Congress was the Indian Health Care Improvement Act, S. 522. Nixon was no longer president, and many in Ford's Cabinet urged a veto because it would cost

$1.6 billion over five years. A veto message prepared by the Office of Management and Budget said there were already improvements in the Indian Health Service and there was "no evidence that a vast infusion of funds, such as proposed by S. 522, would achieve better or faster results than are being achieved under orderly program growth." A memo by OMB's deputy director, Paul O'Neill, said that Indian health statistics were "especially in connection with causes of death, e.g., alcoholism, accidents and suicide, associated with reservation social conditions, i.e., poverty, isolation and inadequate housing. Unfortunately, we have not been especially successful in combating alcoholism and suicides in non-reservation areas."

However, several Republican senators – including Kansas' Bob Dole, who was already named as Ford's running mate in the coming presidential election – argued for the legislation. Barry Goldwater wrote the White House: "I don't think there is a person in the world who would doubt the necessity of this bill. The Indian health facilities are disgraceful and the health care delivery system is inadequate at best … I strongly hope the President will go ahead and sign the bill into law."

So did White House staff members, Dr. Ted Marrs, Brad Patterson and Bobbie Greene Kilberg. Mars told O'Neill: "Admittedly, I am biased as a physician in favor of equity in length of life so you will have to excuse my considering the humanitarian aspect along with the budgetary, pragmatic and political. Failure to adjust the present course is in my opinion a flagrant deprivation of human rights in a measurable as well as dramatic way."

In another short memo, Kilberg pressed O'Neill to travel to an Indian health care facility and see it for himself. "Health care for Native American people is not the place to oppose program expansion," she wrote in April 1976.

Rick Lavis also continued to press the White House with Republican reasoning. A White House memo on Aug. 24 reported that Lavis said one of the problems with the opponents inside the Office of Management and Budget and Health, Education and Welfare is that they never worked to improve the bill. "For a long time, staff asked and asked HEW for the opportunity of sitting down together and trying to work out a compromise bill which would meet HEW's (OMB's) objections," the unsigned White House memo said. "Nothing happened; just another negative letter." Lavis warned the White House that Sen. Fannin "is quite ready to say this on the Senate floor. He is disgusted that HEW never responded to the Hill initiatives on the minority side. Lavis says a veto is unsustainable; the President should sign it with a big Rose Garden ceremony and take the issue away from the Democrats."

Another White House operative, Jack Marsh, was even more blunt: "Please be aware that in the Senate there were no votes against the bill and only six votes against it in the House."

HEW had changed its position and now joined the Interior Department in recommending approval. Still OMB wrote a draft veto message.

However, "our counterarguments won the day," Patterson said. "And the legislation was signed by President Ford."

"I am signing S. 522, the Indian Health Care Improvement Act," President Gerald R. Ford wrote on Oct. 1, 1976. "This bill is not without its faults, but after personal review, I have decided that the well-documented needs for improvement in Indian health manpower, services and facilities outweigh the defects in the bill. ... I am signing this bill because of my own conviction that our first Americans should not be last in opportunity."

CHAPTER NINE

A Seat at the Policy Table

Forrest Gerard had a sense that the Senate's window of opportunity would not stay open long. "I figured I had, maybe, a three-to-five-year window before the scene changed in Indian affairs. It was fairly positive from both the Nixon White House and a powerful senator, Henry M. Jackson, throwing his weight and prestige behind constructive Indian policies," he said. "But I always looked to leaving there after about five years, if I lasted that long."

Gerard could see that Jackson was "starting to cool" on American Indians because the general climate had changed. Jackson's home state had become a hotbed of anti-Indian politics. For example, Rep. Lloyd Meeds, the Democrat who was serving in Jackson's former House seat, barely survived what had been previously easy re-election contests. Meeds shifted from a politician who supported tribal interests (even telling his constituents bluntly to get over the Boldt decision) to one that was questioning recent progressive legislation. "I knew what he was doing, trying to protect his base," Gerard said. "But I didn't think tribal leaders understood. He was too far ahead of his district."

The climate was changing in the Senate too. Legislation to extend the time limit on Indian claims, for example, a process that Jackson had been involved with since his House days, had become controversial. Gerard recalls Jackson asking him to see if Sen. Lee Metcalf, a Democrat from Montana, would sponsor the bill, instead of Jackson. "I said something like, it's getting a little hot around here isn't it, or something like that. I knew things were slowing down."

There was also the prospect of a major Senate reorganization – and uncertainty about which committee would have jurisdiction over Indian affairs. The Interior Committee would become the Committee on Energy and Natural Resources in 1977. Indian affairs moved first to a special, or select, committee, becoming a full, permanent committee in 1984.

"I really looked upon the enactment of the Indian Health Care Improvement Act as the capstone to my career on Capitol Hill and started laying the ground work for my departure," Gerard said.

But that preparation was also philosophical. "When mapping out my career in Washington, D.C., I always harbored the idea of proving I could make it in the private sector," Gerard said. After five and one-half years on the Interior committee Gerard had witnessed many types of lobbyists on Capitol Hill, from oil interests, to environmentalists and a wide-range of corporate and public-interest advocates.

But Indian affairs had a different history. Large law firms had become lobbyists, starting with much of the early legislation that involved significant tribal land claims. Those relationships later evolved into broader representation, essentially non-legal work that anyone with the right understanding of the legislative process could also do.

Gerard's idea, one that he had thought about for many years, was that there was an opening for someone to represent tribes before Congress and the executive branch at a significant discount to what attorneys charged. He had essentially done this for the Indian Health Service when he was the legislative liaison in 1967 (although it couldn't be called "lobbying"). He also had a national network of contacts that included government agencies, organizations, Congress and tribes.

Gerard resigned his post on Jackson's staff and opened his own firm, Gerard & Associates, in November 1976. He secured a small Capitol Hill office and set out to give tribes the same sort of legislative representation that top corporations enjoyed.

"The late Del Lovato (chairman of the All Indian Pueblo Council) learned of my plans to leave the committee ... and made it clear they wanted to hire me as soon as I was in business," Gerard said. "They were essentially my first clients." Within a month, Gerard had all the business he could handle as a solo operator. Clients ranged from the Ak Chin Tribal Community in Arizona to Minnesota's Chippewa Tribe.

"Jackson was always gracious to me," Gerard recalled. "He told me what he told every staffer, 'I don't want to see you standing in the back of a room at a hearing. If you need the committee help, it's open.' A couple of times, when we opposed the inclusion of Indians in the Education Department, I went to Jackson and said, 'I personally believe the Indians might be better off, but politically they see it in a different context, the termination process of dismantling.' So Jackson said, 'Tell me what you want me to do.' He was on record opposing it (and the idea died)."

However, Gerard's lobbying enterprise didn't last long. A new president, Jimmy Carter, asked Gerard to join the administration as the first assistant interior secretary for Indian affairs. Gerard said he was intent on continuing with his business, "but in Washington, D.C., ego always gets in the way." He accepted

President Jimmy Carter selects Forrest J. Gerard as the first assistant secretary for Indian affairs in the U.S. Department of the Interior.

the nomination.

Previously the top post in Indian affairs had been the commissioner of Indian affairs, but Carter had made a campaign promise to bring Indian affairs into the top circle of policy discussions.

"You have to understand that under the new arrangement, the assistant secretary for Indian affairs will not be absorbed in the day-to-day operations of the BIA as he will be with overall policy; fighting within the Interior Department, dealing with OMB (the Office of Management and Budget), the Congress and major contacts outside the department," Gerard said on Aug. 26, 1977. Gerard briefed four tribal newspaper editors before his confirmation hearings.

But first, Gerard had to win Senate confirmation – and that meant approval from new Select Committee on Indian Affairs, chaired by South Dakota's Sen. James Abourezk.

"From my standpoint, I really have no interpersonal problems with the senator," Gerard told the tribal journalists. "I've heard second – third – and fourth-hand that the senator has some reservations about my appointment, in the belief that I would not pursue such matters as reorganization and fundamental changes within the BIA as aggressively as he would like."

Gerard downplayed any differences with Abourezk on substance, saying it was much more about style. Nonetheless, Abourezk used Senate rules to delay Gerard's confirmation. "I always figured my hair wasn't long enough and I wasn't militant enough," Gerard joked.

Suzan Shown Harjo, the Cheyenne & Hodulgee Muscogee journalist and political activist who worked for the Carter Campaign on Indian issues, called the incident "unfortunate." She said a lot of momentum was lost on the hill because Abourezk and his allies "were playing out their enemies game. ... It was more than unseemly. It was juvenile. It seemed childish."

Abourezk eventually blinked. Gerard was confirmed – although the relationship did not improve. Abourezk "wanted things to happen right now and they don't in a bureaucracy," Gerard said.

One of Gerard's earliest successes came even before his confirmation. The Carter administration was ready to move ahead with a new national water policy that would have grouped tribal water claims into broader federal water rights. Neither tribes nor the BIA was consulted about the new policy. And the lead appointment to consider Indian water claims was the assistant secretary for reclamation – often a nemesis of the tribal interests.

However Gerard was able to get Interior Secretary Cecil Andrus to step back and change the deal. Even better the assistant secretary for reclamation staff had to rewrite the Federal Register announcement adding Indian Affairs to the policy discussion.

The Carter water policy opened up the possibility for negotiated settlements by the tribes while preserving the option of litigation (which often meant years or decades in court).

Gerard said this demonstrated the importance of the assistant secretary for Indian affairs as a post to influence policy.

Another example of Gerard's policy role was another fight over Northwest treaty fishing rights. Washington Sen. Warren Magnuson and his staff proposed legislation that would have created a federal commission to regulate fishing. There were representatives from the Departments of the Interior, Commerce, the Sierra Club, commercial and sports fishing interests.

Gerard told Secretary Andrus (before accepting the assistant secretary post) that it would be a deal breaker if Indian Affairs were not included in what had become a political "stacked deck." Robert Herbst, the assistant secretary for fish, wildlife and parks, agreed and volunteered to step off the committee in favor of Gerard.

"We literally turned around the administration on a bill to strip the Boldt decision," Gerard said.

Sen. Jackson played a quiet part in this dispute, as well. Early in the process Interior official John Hough told Jackson about Senator Magnuson's idea for a resolution on a drive from Seattle to Olympia. Jackson listened to the presentation, then just before leaving the car, he asked Hough how the administration proposed resolving a Fifth Amendment taking of the tribe's treaty right? End of discussion.

At the White House, those supporting the measure made

their pitch. But Gerard, Interior Solicitor Leo Krulitz and Anne Wexler from the White House argued that overturning the tribe's treaty victory in the Supreme Court wasn't a smart policy decision.

"At the meeting where we turned it around, Anne Wexler came over and the question was asked, 'Who's going to deal with Magnuson?' I remember her saying, 'I'll deal with Maggie.' Very few tribes around the country understood the role Indian Affairs played in stopping that effort to undercut a very important treaty right," Gerard said.

Gerard also faced operational challenges at the Bureau of Indian Affairs. The Congress was not satisfied with the agency's ability to track spending. This was before the era of self-determination when tribes could contract to operate government programs. "The BIA was a surrogate government for tribes, running everything. It was a microcosm of the U.S. government," said Gerard. The BIA contracted with Price Waterhouse to launch the Management Improvement Project to start reviewing the agency's financial infrastructure.

Gerard returned to his private enterprise in 1980, first with Gerard, Byler & Associates, then his own firm, and finally a partnership with his former colleague in the House, Franklin Ducheneaux.

"I was anxious to get out, to prove that I could make it in the private sector," Gerard said. "Here again we had all the clients we could handle in a short period of time," including Colville, the Minnesota Chippewa Tribe and the Ak-Chin Community.

If there's a theme to Gerard's career on the Hill, in the executive branch and in his own firms, it is his relentless drive to find practical solutions to historical problems. The settlement of the Ak-Chin water claims is a prime example. The community could have litigated, held out for a court victory that could have come in some 30, 40 or even 50 years out. But the leadership, working with Gerard, opted instead for a negotiated settlement with Congress that entitled the Ak-Chin Community to 75,000 acre-feet of Colorado River water. This was a long process that began shortly after Gerard left the Interior Committee and was finally resolved in 1984. It was also a bipartisan deal: Conservative Interior Secretary James Watt (an attorney himself) saw the benefits of negotiated solution and was able to use his authority to find uncommitted water on the Central Arizona Project to make it so.

Gerard summed up his philosophy about lobbying in an interview in 1992 with Indian Country Today:

"If you're going to specialize in lobbying in Indian affairs, it's absolutely critical that you know the history of federal Indian relations and the policies that are in existence and the new policies that are needed. And the other critical ingredient is that you have to have some understanding of the legislative process. You just can't go to D.C. and set up a shingle and say, 'I'm going to be a lobbyist.' That's a distinct process. You've got to know when to intervene, got to have a good sense of timing. You've got to understand that much of that work in the legislative process is conducted by staff, and it's important that you be able to develop rapport with key staffers. In fact, I used to tell my clients, 'It doesn't bother me if I never see a member of Congress as long as we have the staffer who has the word on our issue.' ... Those are the kinds of fundamentals that I've tried to convey to people; and having a good understanding of governmental structure, how policy decisions are made, the relationships between the secretariats, say, of Interior, OMB [Office of Management and Budget] and the Congress."

CHAPTER TEN

A Hard, Tough Fight, Everywhere

There is the cynical view of Henry M. Jackson and his work on American Indian legislation during the 1970s. The narrative goes like this: Jackson wanted to run for president – and so he tossed termination aside and used Indian issues as his platform.

The only part of that story that fits with the facts is that Jackson did run for president. Twice. First he campaigned in the 1972 Democratic Party primaries and then again four years later.

"This is going to be a hard, tough fight, everywhere," Jackson told his supporters when he launched his first campaign. "We've got some hard, tough issues that need to be articulated and I think there's been too much silence in some areas."

Indian issues were areas of policy where there was too much silence. That's why the logic of Jackson using Indians as a prop for the presidency works so well. This narrative builds on the context of Richard Nixon and Jackson as competitors, the notion that Jackson did not want to be outflanked by Nixon on the left. After all, Nixon directly challenged Jackson and his Interior Committee over the return of New Mexico's Blue Lake to the Taos Pueblo.

Nixon considered Jackson his most formidable opponent for

the presidency. He also considered Jackson the most effective Democrat in the Senate and an ally on most international and military matters. One clear measure of that respect was on the Blue Lake matter. Nixon told domestic counselor John Ehrlichman that if the White House was taking on Jackson – they had better win.

The idea of a Jackson campaign using Indian issues even had backing from his supporters and staff. Forrest Gerard recalls that the Jackson advisers who interviewed him for the staff position on the committee were quite open about the politics in question.

And now the story of Jackson's motivation is told in nearly every account about that era. It's a story that's stuck in historical cement.

The Menominee cause was fortunate when "in 1972 Henry Jackson decided to run for president. Needing to appeal to a national constituency (one increasingly sympathetic to Indians), he gave his full support to Menominee restoration," wrote Charles Wilkinson in his book, "Blood Struggle."

Historian Thomas Clarkin's book, "Federal Indian Policy in the Kennedy and Johnson Administrations" also dismisses Jackson's Indian policy because it "proved to be one of cynicism and self-promotion." But there is no proof, no evidence that Jackson linked Indian issues with his presidential campaign. What is interesting is the source of this story. In Clarkin's book it was an unidentified Senate Interior Committee staff member who said: "Some of his later actions in the early '70s clouded the Scoop Jackson that we knew in the '60s because 'what he did was calculated, and was measured against what he could gain from the standpoint of the old 1600 Pennsylvania position.' Thus, Jackson's new attitude toward Indian affairs was part of his bid for the White House rather than a sincere response to Native American needs."

The source is important because the senator's work on Indian issues was a repudiation of the Interior Committee on termination. The senator was saying, in effect, that his actions during the '60s were wrong – and that would be a direct criticism on the unnamed staff members who were critical of Jackson's "calculated" move.

The narrative also falls apart when you examine Jackson's record. There was no action, no speech and no use of any Indian-related issue in either of Scoop's presidential campaigns. This was an area of silence – at least on Scoop's part.

Hank Adams, an Assiniboine, who lived at Frank's Landing near Olympia and was active in the fishing rights disputes in Washington, formed a group of young Northwest American Indians to campaign against Jackson. "Senator Jackson has accomplished more for 53,000 employees of the Boeing Corporation than he has been willing to advocate for a comparable number of Alaskan Natives," Adams told the American Indian Press Association.

On the other hand, in 1972 both Sen. George McGovern and President Nixon formed Indian advisory teams and released papers touting their positions on Indian affairs. So did candidates Jimmy Carter and Gerald Ford four years later. But no such organization was created for Jackson's 1972 or 1976 campaigns.

Abe Bergman said he urged Jackson to cite his record in the Democratic primaries where it could disarm some of the senator's liberal critics. "Why don't you use your Indian legislation?" Bergman asked. "This happened to be in the Massachusetts primary where there were a lot of liberals. Wouldn't it blow away the liberals to let them know what you've done for Indian people? He wouldn't do it. Forrest and I both went to talk to him about it. He didn't say no. He said, 'Well, OK, that's interesting.' But he never did anything."

Jackson just wasn't that type of politician. "His presidential campaign, in retrospect, was a joke because he didn't know how to do (things like) sound bites," Bergman said. "Jackson didn't have good political judgment." But that's often how he operated. After sponsoring the National Health Service Corps legislation, for example, Bergman suggested he take credit. Jackson's support of the legislation was critical because of his military expertise and his place at the Democratic Party's political center. No. " 'Health is Maggie's thing, Maggie takes care of health.' He wouldn't intrude; he wouldn't talk about himself," Bergman said. "That's why I say he's a bad politician. Forrest and I were really disappointed that he wouldn't talk about Indian legislation."

There was another important political consideration: Jackson was not alone in his early support for termination. It was common. The list of termination supporters in the 1960s was a roster of the Senate. It was accepted as a benevolent policy.

"Remember at that time almost everyone in Congress was a terminationist ... pick a senator – and that was their inclination," said Suzan Shown Harjo, who covered Jackson for the American Indian Press Association and later worked as executive director of the National Congress of American Indians.

Bergman said looking back it's easy to see termination as punitive and disastrous. "We know it's wrong now, but good people supported the concept," he said. "People like Hubert Humphrey supported termination, without knowing the consequences, it sounded good."

Henry M. Jackson visiting with totem pole carvers in Washington, D.C.

There might have been another reason for Jackson's support of termination. Like many American Indians, Jackson's Norwegian family had to reach its own conclusion about cultural assimilation. "He respected his parents' heritage, culture and the language being part of that culture, but he discovered personally he had to be proficient in the English language because that was the language spoken in business and other circles," said Gerard. That was not any different from American Indian parents, including Gerard's own, who saw the adoption of English as the route to success.

Termination was an extension of the logic of assimilation.

American Indian issues never surfaced as part of Jackson's bid for the presidency – or at home in Washington. Robert Dellwo, the attorney for the Spokane Tribe, sent a letter to Scoop in 1967 suggesting he use a picture of a tribal visit to his

Spokane Tribal Chairman Alex Sherwood and tribal attorney Robert Dellwo meeting with Henry M. Jackson (center).

office for campaign material. "You have no idea how impressive these pictures were to the members of the tribe at a general tribal report meeting," Dellwo wrote. Jackson responded that he'd like to send autographed copies of the picture to the other members of the council. No mention, and likely, no thought about a campaign use.

In a March 1975 interview with Terry Tafoya and the Northwest Indian News, Jackson made no mention of his initiatives on self-determination or health care. But he did talk about the complexity of solving treaty-fishing disputes after the 1974 Boldt decision. U.S. District Judge George Boldt, the author of the decision, was unpopular in many circles in a state so divided that it was sometimes called "the Mississippi of Indian Country." There was even a proposal on the ballot to abrogate or rewrite treaties, a notion that Washington voters rejected.

But Jackson was as careful as a politician can be when answering questions about treaty fishing rights. "I would support any move to bring about a resolution of the problem to prevent an ongoing protraction of it, which is very destabilizing and I think bad because it leads to a whole series of confrontations and uncertainty, which leads to a bad atmosphere and undesirable environment," Jackson told the intertribal monthly newspaper. "I have special concern because I am co-author of the Indian Claims Commission Act of 1946, which gave to Indians the first forum to bring suits for violation of treaties. Prior to that they had to get a private relief bill in every case. So I have a deep interest."

He said it was "imponderable" to consider rewriting every treaty. "What we ought to look for is the shortest, quickest, fairest, most equitable way of resolving the dispute."

Tafoya's article said that Jackson was "using the interview as an opportunity to blow his own horn" by talking about the Indian Claims Commission. But also interesting is what the senator did not talk about to pitch his presidential bid. The Senate had already passed the Indian Health Care Improvement Act and was nearly ready to do so again. He could have mentioned removing James Gamble from his Interior Committee role, hiring Forrest Gerard or his support for several pieces of legislation in the works. But Jackson remained silent on this front.

However, other presidential candidates, ones with far less substantial records, were eager to talk about federal-Indian policy.

In the 1972 election, both George McGovern and Richard Nixon formed Native American committees as well as highlighting the American Indian and Alaska Native delegates at the conventions. McGovern even credited Indian voters with his first win. "In 1962, when he won his first Senate seat by the slenderest of slender margins – only 597 votes – South Dakota's voting Indian population was solidly in his corner," wrote Richard LaCourse for the American Indian Press Association. "In a traditionally Republican state, McGovern – who built the Democratic Party there into a humming political machine – was the first Democratic senator from the state in 26 years. The victory is being accepted now by his aides as an index of McGovern's indebtedness to his Indian electorate."

McGovern's record was contradictory. He was one of the first in the Senate to abandon termination, beginning with his sponsorship of a 1966 resolution to that end. He also supported the Taos Pueblo in their quest for Blue Lake's return.

"McGovern's Indian critics discuss his absenteeism from regular Senate subcommittee working sessions on pivotal reform Indian legislation, and his frequent absences during critical floor votes in the Senate," wrote LaCourse. "They question whether he has used his chairmanship on the Indian affairs subcommittee to its fullest in serving the legislative needs of Indians."

Back in South Dakota, there is "some disenchantment with him on the part of Indians who believe that once he won his Senate seat he lost his working concern for Indian needs and, instead devoted himself to 'national issues.' Consequently," LaCourse wrote, "he has a credibility problem with the Indians at home."

However, McGovern had no qualms about citing Indian affairs in his campaign. In April 1972, he pledged to offer two administrative alternatives to the Bureau of Indian Affairs. "The two options are placement of the BIA under the Executive Office of the President or the choice of Cabinet status," according to the American Indian Press Association. McGovern dismissed the Nixon adminstration as "high on promises, but short on performance."

The Nixon-Agnew ticket said it would build on its record. A message signed by Richard Nixon to the National Tribal Chairmen's Association said: "Our policy, as you know, is firm and unwavering: Greater self-determination so that America's Indians can manage their own affairs."

Nixon said he had already delivered on that promise. "We have returned certain lands to the Indian people as one proof of our unbending intent that self-determination becomes a reality. We have further backed this intent with legislation that we have twice urged the Congress to pass. We will continue to urge the passage of these laws which are so vital to the fulfillment of the aspirations of American Indians."

But the Nixon record was more complex. LaCourse wrote: "Speculation is rife here that Indian Commissioner Louis R. Bruce will be dismissed if the Nixon administration wins re-election in November and that speculation is already affecting the subtle atmosphere of the Bureau." LaCourse was right. A few weeks after the election, Bruce was fired.

Democrats and the Republican president cited their Indian record at some point during the long campaign season. Even Hubert Humphrey was on record with an Indian policy statement. But LaCourse pointed out there was a problem. The former vice president had promised Minnesota tribes to "add a capable Indian to his Washington staff to coordinate Indian interests and his own efforts. To date, none has been hired."

There are many reasons to discount Jackson's supposed cynical use of Indian affairs as a campaign tool.

First, Jackson's legislative record was a quiet success. Gerard and Rick Lavis said they were more occupied by the bipartisan mechanics of getting a bill through Congress rather than seeking publicity.

"Why didn't we toot our own horn?" Lavis asked. "Well, if anyone was going to be out there tooting the horn it was Sen. Jackson and political leaders. What Forrest and I were in charge of was getting the bill done. Forrest and I weren't given to publicity. We just had a job to do."

Jackson was silent on his Indian record, too. Then he had a reputation as a lousy politician. Jackson just wasn't your back-slapping best friend in Washington. He was a serious, thoughtful leader. Indeed, Jackson's journey away from the termination policy into his role as a champion for self-determination occurred over decades (rather than during a campaign cycle). Jackson once thought, incorrectly, that termination worked. But he wasn't the first Democrat to see termination as a mistake – and certainly not the last. Frank Church, for example, reached the same conclusion much later. More than that, Jackson found a way to deliver on his promises. While other politicians had pledged to hire Native Americans on Capitol Hill, Jackson did so. But he didn't hire a token. He hired a staff member that he could trust, Forrest Gerard, and then let Gerard engage in the real reform effort. And all this was put into place without the fanfare associated with a presidential campaign or, for that matter, history.

CHAPTER ELEVEN

Legacy

The Senate of Henry M. Jackson was a very different place from the one we know today. The building is the same, most of the rules are the same, but the way the people's business was conducted was more courtly, formal and less partisan.

These days Jackson is remembered as a special kind of politician. He was a philosopher, an advocate for a strong military presence by the United States, and the author of modern environmental laws. He was also half of a powerful pair of U.S. senators from Washington, the junior partner to Warren Grant "Maggie" Magnuson.

"I was interested in politicians. Who they really were. How they lived their lives. Magunson and Jackson were so different as people," said Dr. Abe Bergman, who had worked with both senators on health issues. The key to Jackson was his nature. "He really was this Norwegian, moral, prototype of a kid from Everett who delivered newspapers every day," Bergman said. "That's how he got his name, 'Scoop.' Jackson liked diving deep into issues. He really wanted to understand them, almost as if he were a university professor and not a U.S. senator."

Washington's two senators were called (by critics and friends alike) the "the gold-dust twins" or the "senators from Boeing." They had a reputation as being especially expert at securing federal dollars for their state. Perhaps their power was best summed up by then-Vice President Walter Mondale during a 1977 stop in Seattle. He told reporters he was worried that Maggie, the chairman of the Appropriations Committee, would abuse his spending powers. Mondale paused, then added, but "Maggie said he'd thought about it and, to be fair, would apportion the money 50-50. That's 50 percent for Washington and 50 percent for the rest of the country."

While Jackson and Magnuson worked together as a team on many issues, they were dissimilar as individuals. Maggie held court, usually a drink in hand, most evenings in his Capitol Hill office. Jackson, on the other hand, won one of his first elections with the nickname of "Soda Pop" because of his enforcement of strict gambling and liquor rules as well as his scarce inclination to engage in drink. Jackson's reputation was frugal and hard-working.

But it was an era when the senators worked together, freely giving credit for good work as much as demanding it.

As Suzan Shown Harjo, who was following much of this legislation for the American Indian Press Association, said, the old Senate was about "governing." The style was more civil, even the word "I" was discouraged as bragging. "There was as much animosity then as today," Harjo said. "But people had greater self-control."

Jackson's shift from termination is a case in point. Lucy Covington, the leader of the Colvilles who fought termination, didn't give up on Jackson when he supported termination. She "moved him from neutral to more on her side neutral," Harjo said. Jackson's record supports that, because his move was more of an evolution of thought rather than an epiphany (complicated by his relationship with his mentor, Clinton Anderson).

Contrast that with the way tribes treated Sen. Slade Gorton in the 1980s and 1990s. Like Jackson, he was viewed as a modern Custer, but Washington tribes worked to defeat him at the ballot – a successful venture – rather than converting him. The two politicians started with different philosophies, but the difference reflects the growing political power of tribes.

One of those differences, and perhaps why Covington and others continued to work with Jackson, is that he had a remarkable ability to quietly shift his positions. He listened, examined the facts and then judged the situation on its merits in the same solemn fashion as a judge.

For example, not long after the return of Blue Lake to the Taos Pueblo, the Yakama Nation demanded the return of Mount Adams. This situation was similar in the sense that the United States was incontrovertibly in the wrong. A surveyor's mistake had moved tribal land into what became a national forest.

Richard LaCourse, a tribal member, wrote that the Yakamas considered Mount Adams a holy place. "The mountain still stands at the center of their religion. First among the region's peaks to be graced by light at sunrise since it lies in the East, *Pahto* is viewed as an emblem … of the people's spirit."

The Yakama refused Indian Claims Commission money and demanded their land back; the Forest Service said its return would "restrict public use."

President Richard Nixon signed an executive order returning the land on May 20, 1972. Jackson supported the move.

A second example is that of Fort Lawson on Seattle's Magnolia Bluff. Shortly after the base was decommissioned, Jackson stood with city leaders and pledged to find a way to make it a park. But American Indians and Alaska Natives in Seattle, led by Bernie Whitebear, had a different plan for the facility. The

Henry M. Jackson and Warren G. Magnuson were called the "gold dust twins" because of their reputation as being experts at securing federal dollars for their state.

group took over the facility and said the area tribes had first right to reacquire the land. In the legislation that turned over title to most of the park to Seattle, Jackson required a 20-acre preserve for Whitebear's United Indians of All Tribes Foundation. Today Seattle's urban Indian population boasts of a land-based home with the Daybreak Star Center as the community's gathering place.

In June 1975, when Jackson received an award from the National Congress of American Indians, he said this about the legacy of self-determination: "Unless we are wiling to give tribes the opportunity to perform bona fide governmental functions, they stand no chance of growing beyond the paper entities that they represent today." The Indian Self-Determination and Educational Assistance Act "provides the Bureau of Indian Affairs and the Indian Health Service with a new mandate – one that ends the last vestiges of their role as 19th century colonial institutions and one which makes them true advocates of Indian tribes."

But what did colonialism mean in a 20th century context? Simply this: The Bureau of Indian Affairs was the government for Indian communities. The BIA "doled out welfare, managed the natural resources and managed the health care. They were the show on the reservation," said Forrest Gerard. The new self-determination law sent a message to tribes that "you're here. You have the right to assume control and responsibility for programs and services operated by the BIA and then the IHS on your reservations."

At the same time, the Congress admitted an obligation in the Indian Health Care Improvement Act with a finding that "federal health services to maintain and improve the health of Indians are consonant with and required by the federal government's historical and unique legal relationship ... and a major national goal of the United States is to provide the quantity and quality of health services which will permit the health status of Indians to be raised to the highest possible level and to encourage the maximum participation of Indians in the planning and management of those services."

In other words, the new law shifted the say to tribes. It was up to tribes, not the secretary of Interior or Health and Human Services, to make the call about receiving federal services or being ready to provide those governmental services directly.

Jackson must have understood the historical nature of his legislation. The senator once asked Gerard if he thought tribal contracting under self-determination would quickly absorb most government programs. "No," Gerard told him, there would be "steady progress."

The record bears that out. Tribal contracts under self-determination and self-governance (a 1980s addition to the program) have restructured both the Bureau of Indian Affairs and the Indian Health Service into funding agencies as much as government programs. Roughly half of the BIA's $2.2 billion annual budget is transferred to tribes through contracts. And some 40 percent of the IHS' $ 3.8 billion annual budget is now under local control. Tribes and Alaska Native corporations administer 14 hospitals, 240 health centers, 102 health stations and 166 Alaska village clinics.

But those are just numbers. If one really wants to understand the impact of self-determination, spend 30 seconds walking about the Alaska Native Medical Center in Anchorage. A visit to the campus shows the legacy of self-determination in absolute terms because government money is used to fund a health program designed and operated by Alaska Natives. There are values communicated in every hallway. Colorful banners remind visitors that the entire campus is tobacco free; There are many gathering places scattered about for family and community with the finest in traditional art showcased; and, in waiting areas, there are open computer terminals for people to research their own health information. Signs remind patients that if you've been waiting more than 15 minutes, talk to someone.

The conversation between Jackson and Gerard predicted a steady progress on tribal control. This is the evidence: The Alaska Native Medical Center includes a model outpatient facility operated by the Southcentral Foundation, the non-profit affiliate of the Cook Inlet Region Inc., one of the corporations set up

Forrest J. Gerard now lives in Albuquerque, N.M.

under the Alaska Native Claims Settlement Act. Southcentral assumed the operations for Indian Health Service programs in 1987 and by 1999 ran the whole show. A little more than a decade later, Southcentral serves 55,000 people (including 10,000 people in 55 remote villages) with its 1,400 employees.

"I believe that Alaska is the only state that has enacted Indian self-determination to the fullest extent of the law in assuming health care," says Katherine Gottlieb, president and chief executive officer of the Southcentral Foundation. "We have taken what we had from the government and transformed it."

It's not just federal programs managed by a native organization; instead, the federal money is redesigned to build a system based on Alaska Native ownership. So much so that Southcentral Foundation continually refers to its "customer/owners" as its foundation and inspiration.

In this case, self-determination means just that. Alaska Natives and American Indian tribal groups are using Jackson's legacy of self-determination to redefine what works best in a community.

Joseph Kalt, the Ford Foundation professor of International Political Economy at Harvard, testified to the Senate Committee on Indian Affairs on Sept. 27, 2000, that the research backs up the Jackson-Gerard approach. "Self-determination is the only policy in a century that has worked to begin to alleviate the legacy of suppression and economic dependency to which Native people in the U.S. have been subjected," he said. Kalt runs the Harvard Project on American Indian Economic Development at the John F. Kennedy School of Government. "It is no coincidence that Indian Country is now dotted with an increasing number of reservations where economic development is taking hold. From Flathead and Grand Ronde to Mississippi Choctaw, Grand Traverse and Citizen Potawatomi, sustained economic development has taken hold. Improvement in economic conditions at such reservations, moreover, has been accompanied by improved social conditions."

MARK TRAHANT PHOTO

Katherine Gottlieb, MBA, is president and chief executive officer of the Southcentral Foundation. The foundation contracts with the Indian Health Service to jointly operate the Alaska Native Medical Center practicing self-determination.

There are two other themes from this era that ought to be considered as part of the Jackson and Gerard legacies.

The first was the way Jackson hired people. Looking at the record, it's no accident that he hired Forrest Gerard. The senator was methodical in his approach to finding talent on Capitol Hill. He had hired Thomas Foley Jr. before he ran for Congress. And Bill Van Ness was identified as a promising University of Washington law school student.

"I didn't have a job at the time because I had a Sterling fellowship to go to Yale Law School and do graduate work, and what I wanted to do was to be a law professor," Van Ness said. Jackson called and asked him to interview for a special counsel job, even though Van Ness had no interest in going to Washington, D.C. "We had two kids at the time, a broken-down station wagon and lots of bills from going to school, so I did talk to him. I found him to be a charming, highly intellectual guy and

I liked him."

Gerard's hiring was similar. Van Ness said they had seen Gerard operate on Capitol Hill and were impressed. Once hired, Jackson's trust in Gerard developed quickly.

"Forrest was not a bullshit artist. He wasn't a young guy, he knew his way around," Van Ness said. "He didn't waste Scoop's time. His memos were short, sharp and to the point."

Van Ness and Gerard often worked out the policy between them. "And if Forrest and I were on the same page, Scoop didn't see the need to go much further," Van Ness said.

The second theme, also a legacy, is a philosophy about governing, which is to find those solutions that can win enough support to be executed. Both Jackson and Gerard – throughout their careers – were practitioners of this notion and that made the golden era of Indian legislation possible. It could be said that there were better, more progressive proposals over those decades involving Indian issues. There were smart, well-intentioned advocates on every side of these issues. But no matter how strong the argument, no matter how right a tribal point of view might be, it meant nothing if it could not be enacted into law. This is an important message because the craft of governing has become increasingly rare.

Finding politically possible solutions is the essence of the Jackson and Gerard approach to Indian issues. How could the language appeal to Democrats and Republicans enough to pass a bill? Gerard developed a strategy to win – and it's this contribution that, in part, changed the premise of Indian relations. There was a before and after.

Of course everybody does tell a different story about this.

To Forrest Gerard — With admiration
and great respect from his Chairman
1976. Henry M Jackson

AUTHOR'S NOTE

My goal was to keep the foregoing narrative as accessible as possible, so I decided against footnotes. I did, however, try to cite the source material in the text. A series of interviews began with Forrest Gerard on Jan. 15, 2005. Over the next five years they took place at his homes in San Mateo and Albuquerque. I also interviewed for this project Charles Trimble, Philip Sam Deloria, Suzan Shown Harjo, William Van Ness, Rick Lavis, Brad Patterson, Abraham Bergman and Vivian Vahlberg. I also interviewed the late John Ehrlichman about the Nixon administration's role in Indian affairs in Santa Fe, N.M., in 1987.

I have also collected dispatches from the American Indian Press Association. The AIPA was a full news service operating in Washington, D.C., from 1971 through 1975.

Additional source material includes tribal newspapers: The Collville Tribune, American Indian Affairs, Wassaja, Akwesasne Notes, Northwest Indian News, Tundra Times, Our Heritage and the Yakama Nation Review. I also included material from Senator Jackson's office, including press releases from the Jackson archives at the University of Washington.

ACKNOWLEDGMENTS

It's important to start my "thank you" list with a debt of gratitude. I'm delighted to have had the opportunity to write about Forrest Gerard. He has been my friend and mentor for more than 30 years. I first met Gerard in 1977 when I was the editor of my tribal newspaper, The Sho-Ban News, after I had written editorials blasting the assistant secretary for Indian affairs for this or that policy decision (I am not even sure what the issues were back then). Gerard suggested we meet. I remember being impressed by his thoughtful, deliberative approach to complex policy questions. Even better, he could explain his thinking in clear terms – an ideal source for a young journalist. A few years later, I went to work for Gerard and the Bureau of Indian Affairs. My government career lasted about a year because I missed the newspaper business too much. But it was through that experience that Gerard became my mentor, one that's made a huge different in my life and career. We have talked regularly on the phone for more than 30 years, often about politics, but also about family and career. Because of that relationship – and my admiration for what Gerard has been able to do in public service – I wanted to tell the stories in this book.

I also want to acknowledge the Henry M. Jackson Foundation and the Seattle Indian Health Board for financial and logistical support. The Jackson Foundation provided a generous grant for research and production. I'd especially like to thank Bill Van Ness, Lara Iglitzin and Laura Mapp. Ralph Forquera of the Seattle Indian Health Board was a terrific partner – and a first-rate sounding board for many of the ideas in the book.

This project was also possible because of my fellowship with the Kaiser Family Foundation. A special thanks to Penny Duckham.

I visited and benefited from the collections at the American Native Press Archives and Sequoyah Research Center at the University of Arkansas – Little Rock. The center is a rich repository for American Indian and Alaska Native tribal newspapers and other documents and director Daniel Littlefield is a remarkable guide. I also took advantage of White House documents collected by Capt. Allan Dellapenna Jr. who coordinated the Indian Health Service's Gold Book.

I am also grateful for my conversations with Philip Sam Deloria, now at the American Indian Graduate Center in Albuquerque. He has a rich view of history and an expansive approach to these issues.

Thank you to JiaYing Grygiel for the book's design and Merry Nye for copy editing. We worked together at the Seattle Post-Intelligencer – and I am delighted to be on the same team again. I had the pleasure of working again with Marc Jaffe, the book's editor. Every time his pencil touches my words, the ideas get stronger. I look forward to future projects.

Last, but not least, a thank you to my family. First, my wife, Nora, and my boys, Marvin and Elias, because they give me purpose and make the work easy.

Thank you all. I'm a lucky guy.

Mark Trahant

INDEX

SELECTED REFERENCES

Works Cited

Anderson, Clinton P. *Outsider in the Senate: Senator Clinton Anderson's Memoirs.* New York and Cleveland: World Company, 1970. Print.

Arnold, Robert P. *Alaska Natives & The Land.* Washington: U.S. Govt Printing Office, 1968. Print.

Baker, Richard A. *Conservation politics the Senate career of Clinton P. Anderson.* Albuquerque: University of New Mexico, 1985. Print.

Berger, Thomas R. *Village journey the report of the Alaska Native Review Commission.* Rev. ed. New York: Hill and Wang, 1995. Print.

Clarkin, Thomas. *Federal Indian Policy in the Kennedy and Johnson Administrations, 1961-1969.* New York: University of New Mexico, 2001. Print.

Cobb, Daniel M. *Beyond Red Power American Indian Politics and Activism Since 1900.* New York: School for Advanced Research, 2007. Print.

Cohen, Felix S. *Cohen's handbook of federal Indian law.* 2005 ed. ed. Newark, NJ: LexisNexis, 2005. Print.

Deloria Jr., Vine. *We Talk, You Listen.* New York City: MacMillan Company, 1970. Print.

Deloria Jr., and Clifford Lytle. *Nations within the past and future of American Indian sovereignty.* New York: Pantheon, 1984. Print.

Deloria Jr., and David E. Wilkins. *Tribes, Treaties, and Constitutional Tribulations.* New York: University of Texas, 2000. Print.

Deloria Jr., *Custer Died For Your Sins.* New York: Avon, 1970. Print. Particularly useful for overall view of Indian field; termination history

Dippie, Brian W. *The Vanishing American.* Middleton, Connecticut:

Wesleyan UP, 1985. Print.

Edmunds, R. David, ed. *New warriors Native American leaders since 1900*. Lincoln: University of Nebraska, 2001. Print.

Fahey, John. *Saving the reservation Joe Garry and the battle to be Indian*. Seattle, WA: University of Washington, 2001. Print.

Fixico, Donald Lee. *Termination and relocation federal Indian policy, 1945-1960*. 1st ed. ed. Albuquerque: University of New Mexico, 1986. Print.

Frechette, James G. "Termination report (untitled)." Menominee News 3 (23 Mar. 1956): 1. Print. Report by the Chairman of the Menominee Tribe's Advisory Council in the form of a tribal newsletter.

Gordon-McCutchan, R. C. *Taos Indians and the battle for Blue Lake*. Santa Fe, N.M: Red Crane, 1991. Print.

Harris, Fred R. *Does people do it? A memoir*. Norman: University of Oklahoma, 2008. Print.

Harris, LaDonna. *LaDonna Harris A Comanche Life (American Indian Lives)*. New York: Bison, 2006. Print.

The Harvard Project:, Eric C. Henson, Jonathan B. Taylor, Catherine E. A. Curtis, Stephen Cornell, Kenneth W. Grant, Miriam R. Jorgensen, Joseph P. Kalt, and Andrew J. Lee. *The State of the Native Nations Conditions under U.S. Policies of Self-Determination*. New York: Oxford UP, USA, 2007. Print.

Hensley, William L. Iggiagruk. *Fifty miles from tomorrow a memoir of Alaska and the real people*. New York: Farrar, Straus and Giroux, 2008. Print.

Hoff, Joan. *Nixon Reconsidered*. New York: Basic Bks., 1995. Print.

Hurtado, Albert L., and Peter Iverson, eds. *Major problems in American Indian history documents and essays*. Lexington, Mass: D.C. Heath and, 1994. Print.

Iverson, Peter. *We are still here American Indians in the twentieth century*. Wheeling, Ill: Harlan Davidson, 1998. Print.

Josephy Jr., Alvin M. *Red Power*. Lincoln and London: Bison, University of Nebraska, 1971. Print.

Kaufman, Robert Gordon. *Henry M. Jackson a life in politics*. Seattle: University of Washington, 2000. 201-01. Print. This biography is a good overview of the senator's life and career. It does – in a paragraph or two – mention his Indian affairs record. Indian Claims Commission Act of 1946. p 31 Indian Education Act of 1972, p. 201 Fort Lawton, Alaska.

Kelly, Lawrence C. *Assault on assimilation John Collier and the origins of Indian policy reform.* Albuquerque: University of New Mexico, 1983. Print.

McNickle, D'arcy. *"Alaska – Getting Acquainted."* Indians at Work 15 Nov. 1936: 5-7. Newsletter.

McNickle, D'Arcy. *Native American Tribalism: Indian Survivals and Renewals.* New York: Oxford UP, 1973. Print.

Nash, Gerald D. *American West transformed the impact of the Second World War.* Bloomington: Indiana UP, 1985. Print.

Olson, James S., and Raymond Wilson. *Native Americans in the twentieth century.* Urbana and Chicago: University of Illinois, 1986. Print.

Parman, Donald Lee. *Indians and the American West in the twentieth century.* Bloomington: Indiana UP, 1994. Print.

Philip, Kenneth R. *Termination revisited American Indians on the trail to self-determination, 1933-1953.* Lincoln: University of Nebraska, 1999. 16-33. Print. Chapter dealing with the Indian Claims Commission is particularly useful for Jackson project. Role of Jackson as House IA chairman, then author of legislation. National hearings and testimony.

Prochnau, William W., and Richard W. Larsen. *A certain Democrat: Senator Henry M. Jackson.* Englewood Cliffs, N.J.: Prentice-Hall, 1972. Print.

Redman, Eric. *The Dance of Legislation.* Seattle: University of Washington, 2001. Print.

Reyes, Lawney L. *Bernie Whitebear an urban Indian's quest for justice.* Tucson: University of Arizona, 2006. Print.

Rife, James P., and Capt. Alan J. Dellapenna, Jr. *Caring & Curing.* Washington: Indian Health Service, 2009. Print.

Scinta, Sam. *Spirit & Reason The Vine Deloria, Jr., Reader.* Grand Rapids: Fulcrum, 1999. Print.

States., United. *Indian Claims Commission act hearings before the*

Committee on Indian Affairs, United States Senate, Seventy-fourth
    Congress, first session, on S. 2731 ... June 10 and 17, 1935. [New
    York: AMS, 1976. Print.
Steiner, Stan. *The New Indians*. 1st ed. ed. New York: Harper &
    Row, 1968. Print.
Szasz, Margaret. *Education and the American Indian the road to
    self-determination since 1928*. Albuquerque, NM: University of
    New Mexico, 1999. Print.
Tyler, S. Lyman. *A History of Indian Policy*. Washington: US Dept of
    Interior, 1973. Print.
Tyler, S. Lyman. *A Working Paper on Termination*. 1964. MS. Provo,
    Utah.
United States. Cong. Senate. Special Committee on Investigations.
    *Mismanagement of Indian Health Service, Dept. of Health and
    Human Services*. 101st Cong., 1st sess. S. Rept. 21-391.
    Washington: US Govt Printing Office, 1989. Print.
United States. Select Committee on Indian Affairs. Congressional
    Research Service. *Federal Programs of Assistance to American
    Indians*. By Richard S. Jones. 179th ed. Vol. 48. Washington:
    US Govt Printing Office, 1985. Print. Ser. 0.
US Govt Printing Office. "Hearings before the United States Senate
    Select Committee on Indian Affairs." Proc. of Nomination
    of Forrest J. Gerard to be an Assistant Secretary of the Interior,
    Washington, DC. 907th ed. Vol. 96. Washington: US Govt
    Printing Office, 1977. Print. Ser. 0.
Wilkins, David E. *Uneven ground American Indian sovereignty and
    federal law*. Norman [Okla.]: University of Oklahoma, 2001.
    Print.
Wilkinson, Charles F. *Blood Struggle The Rise of Modern Indian
    Nations*. Boston: W. W. Norton & Company, 2005. Print.
Wilkinson, Charles F. *Messages from Frank's Landing A Story of
    Salmon, Treaties, and the Indian Way*. New York: University of
    Washington, 2000. Print.
Wilkinson, Charles F. *The American West a narrative bibliography and
    a study in regionalism*. Niwot, Colo: University of Colorado,
    1989. Print.

GLOSSARY

American Indians and Alaska Natives is the legal, precise term for the indigenous people in the United States. Often the first question asked is, "Which is better, Native American or American Indian?" I prefer to use, when possible, the tribal affiliation of the person, then American Indian or Alaska Native. Native American is acceptable, but I use it sparingly.

AIM, or the American Indian Movement, began in 1968 in Minneapolis as a coalition against charges of police brutality. The intertribal organization was involved with many demonstrations in the 1970s, including the Trail of Broken Treaties that led to the takeover of the Bureau of Indian Affairs headquarters in 1972. www.aimovement.org

Assimilation is the idea that American Indians would fade into the fabric of the larger society and tribal cultures would disappear or become museum pieces. At various points in U.S. history assimilation was the stated goal of policy toward American Indians and Alaska Natives.

BIA, or the Bureau of Indian Affairs, is the primary agency responsible for implementing federal policy toward American Indians and Alaska Natives. The BIA began in 1824 in the War Department and is now in the Department of the Interior. The BIA provides government services, such as police or schools, directly or through contracts, grants and other agreements to 564 tribes, serving a population of nearly 2 million American Indian and Alaska Natives.

Indian Country Today is a national weekly newspaper owned and operated by the Oneida Nation of New York. The paper began as the Lakota Times published on the Pine Ridge Reservation in South Dakota.

Indian Claims Commission was a judicial panel that heard claims from Indian tribes against the United States. The commission operated from 1946 through 1978 and only paid cash for claims (instead of returning land or property) as the result of stolen lands or broken treaty promises.

IHS, or the Indian Health Service, provides health care services ranging from sanitation to full hospitalization directly or through contracts, grants and other agreements to 564 tribes, serving a population of nearly 2 million American Indian and Alaska Natives in 35 states.

Indian Country is the legal definition of Indian land and reservations controlled under tribal authority.

The IRA, or the Indian Reorganization Act, also known as the Wheeler-Howard Act of 1934, was considered the Indian's version of the New Deal. The law reversed U.S. policies designed to break up reservation lands and authority and encouraged the creation of formal governing constitutions for tribal governments with increased powers of government.

The Meriam Report was a blunt assessment of U.S. government policy toward American Indians. The 1928 report by the Institute for Government Research, now the Brookings Institute, found appalling health and living conditions on Indian reservations.

NCAI, the National Congress of American Indians, is an intertribal policy organization. It was founded in 1944 to counter the threat of termination.

Public Law 83-280 (often just called "280") gave some state governments limited authority to assume civil and criminal jurisdiction over tribal homelands or reservations.

Relocation was a Bureau of Indian Affairs program that began in the 1940s to implement assimilation by moving American Indians off reservations and into urban areas.

Self-determination is the principle that people have the right to govern themselves and their homeland without interference. It applies to Indian Country with the Public Law 93-638, the Indian Self-Determination and Education Assistance Act. That law allows tribes to directly manage and operate government programs with federal funding.

Termination was a U.S. policy to effect assimilation. House Concurrent Resolution 108, passed in 1953, called for an end to the special relationship between tribes and the federal government. The idea was to settle claims with tribal governments and then terminate the federal government's role on reservations. American Indians would then become subject to state laws.

Selected Text From Public Documents

U.S. House of Representatives Concurrent Resolution 108

"Whereas it is the policy of Congress, as rapidly as possible, to make the Indians within the territorial limits of the United States subject to the same laws and entitled to the same privileges and responsibilities as are applicable to other citizens of the United States, to end their status as wards of the United States, and to grant them all of the rights and prerogatives pertaining to American citizenship....

"Resolved by the House of Representatives (the Senate concurring) That it is declared to be the sense of Congress that, at the earliest possible time, all of the Indian tribes...located within the States of California, Florida, New York, and Texas...should be freed from Federal supervision and control and from all disabilities and limitations specifically applicable to Indians...."

Source: U.S. Statutes at Large, 67: B132. 1953

Richard Nixon Special Message to the Congress on Indian Affairs (Abridged)

To the Congress of the United States:

The first Americans – the Indians – are the most deprived and most isolated minority group in our nation. On virtually every scale of measurement – employment, income, education, health – the condition of the Indian people ranks at the bottom.

This condition is the heritage of centuries of injustice. From the time of their first contact with European settlers, the American Indians have been oppressed and brutalized, deprived of their ancestral lands and denied the opportunity to control their own destiny. Even the Federal programs which are intended to meet their needs have frequently proven to be ineffective and demeaning.

But the story of the Indian in America is something more than the record of the white man's frequent aggression, broken agreements, intermittent remorse and prolonged failure. It is a record also of endurance, of survival, of adaptation and creativity in the face of overwhelming obstacles. It is a record of enormous contributions to this country–to its art and culture, to its strength and spirit, to its sense of history and its sense of purpose.

It is long past time that the Indian policies of the Federal government began to recognize and build upon the capacities and insights of the Indian people. Both as a matter of justice and as a matter of enlightened social policy, we must begin to act on the basis of what the Indians themselves have long been telling us. The time has come to break decisively with the past and to create the conditions for a new era in which the Indian future is determined by Indian acts and Indian decisions.

Self-determination without Termination

The first and most basic question that must be answered with respect to Indian policy concerns the historic and legal relationship between the Federal government and Indian communities. In the past, this relationship has oscillated between two equally harsh and unacceptable extremes.

On the one hand, it has–at various times during previous Administrations-been the stated policy objective of both the Executive and Legislative branches of the Federal government eventually to terminate the trusteeship relationship between the Federal government and the Indian people. As recently as August of 1953, in House Concurrent Resolution 108, the Congress declared that termination was the long-range goal of its Indian policies. This would mean that Indian tribes would eventually lose any special standing they had under Federal law: the tax exempt status of their lands would be discontinued; Federal responsibility for their economic and social well-being would be repudiated; and the tribes themselves would be effectively dismantled. Tribal property would be divided among individual members who would then be assimilated into the society at large.

This policy of forced termination is wrong, in my judgment, for a number of reasons. First, the premises on which it rests are wrong. Termination implies that the Federal government has taken on a trusteeship responsibility for Indian communities as an act of generosity toward a disadvantaged people and that it can therefore discontinue this responsibility on a unilateral basis whenever it sees fit. But the unique status of Indian tribes does not rest on any premise such as this. The special relationship between Indians and the Federal government is the result instead of solemn obligations, which have been entered into by the United States Government. Down through the years, through written treaties and through formal and informal agreements, our government has made specific commitments to the Indian people. For their part, the Indians have often surrendered claims to vast tracts of land and have accepted life on government reservations. In exchange, the government has agreed to provide community services such as health, education and public safety, services which would presumably allow Indian communities to enjoy a standard of living comparable to that of other Americans.

This goal, of course, has never been achieved. But the special relationship between the Indian tribes and the Federal government which arises from these agreements continues to carry immense moral and legal force. To terminate this relationship would be no more appropriate than to terminate the citizenship rights of any other American.

The second reason for rejecting forced termination is that the practical results have been clearly harmful in the few instances in which termination actually has been tried. The removal of Federal trusteeship responsibility has produced considerable disorientation among the affected Indians and has left them unable to relate to a myriad of Federal, State and local assistance efforts. Their economic and social condition has often been worse after termination than it was before.

The third argument I would make against forced termination concerns the effect it has had upon the overwhelming majority of tribes which still enjoy a special relationship with the Federal government. The very threat that this relationship may someday be ended has created a great deal of apprehension among Indian groups and this apprehension, in turn, has had a blighting effect on tribal progress. Any step that might result in greater social, economic or political autonomy is regarded with suspicion by many Indians who fear that it will only bring them closer to the day when the Federal government will disavow its responsibility and cut them adrift.

In short, the fear of one extreme policy, forced termination, has often worked to produce the opposite extreme: excessive dependence on the Federal government. In many cases this dependence is so great that the Indian community is almost entirely run by outsiders who are responsible and responsive to Federal officials in Washington, D.C., rather than to the communities they are supposed to be serving. This is the second of the two harsh approaches which have long plagued our Indian policies. Of the Department of the Interior's programs directly serving Indians, for example, only 1.5 percent are presently under Indian control. Only 2.4 percent of HEW's Indian health programs are run by Indians. The result is a burgeoning Federal bureaucracy, programs which are far less effective than they ought to be, and an erosion of Indian initiative and morale.

I believe that both of these policy extremes are wrong. Federal termination errs in one direction; Federal paternalism errs in the other. Only by clearly rejecting both of these extremes can we achieve a policy which truly serves the best interests of the Indian people. Self-determination among the Indian people can and must be encouraged without the threat of eventual termination. In my view, in fact, that is the only way that self-determination can effectively be fostered.

This, then, must be the goal of any new national policy toward the Indian people: to strengthen the Indian's sense of autonomy without threatening his sense of community. We must assure the Indian that he can assume control of his own life without being separated involuntarily from the tribal group. And we must make it clear that Indians can become independent of Federal control without being cut off from Federal concern and Federal support.

More Money for Indian Health

Despite significant improvements in the past decade and a half, the health of Indian people still lags 20 to 25 years behind that of the general population. The average age at death among Indians is 44 years, about one-third less than the national average. Infant mortality is nearly 50% higher for Indians and Alaska natives than for the population at large; the tuberculosis rate is eight times as high and the suicide rate is twice that of the general population. Many infectious diseases such as trachoma and dysentery that have all but disappeared among other Americans continue to afflict the Indian people.

This Administration is determined that the health status of the first Americans will be improved. In order to initiate expanded efforts in this area, I will request the allocation of an additional $10 million for Indian health programs for the current fiscal year. This strengthened Federal effort will enable us to address ourselves more effectively to those health problems which are particularly important to the Indian community. We understand, for example, that areas of greatest concern to Indians include the prevention and control of alcoholism, the promotion of mental health and the control of middle ear disease. We hope that the ravages of middle-ear disease–a particularly acute disease among Indians–can be brought under control within five years.

These and other Indian health programs will be most effective if more Indians are involved in running them. Yet-almost unbelievably–we are presently able to identify in this country only 30 physicians and fewer than 400 nurses of Indian descent. To meet this situation, we will expand our efforts to train Indians for health careers.

Helping Urban Indians

Our new census will probably show that a larger proportion of America's Indians are living off the reservation than ever before in our history. Some authorities even estimate that more Indians are living in cities and towns than are remaining on the reservation. Of those American Indians who are now dwelling in urban areas, approximately three-fourths are living in poverty.

The Bureau of Indian Affairs is organized to serve the 462,000 reservation Indians. The BIA's responsibility does not extend to Indians who have left the reservation, but this point is not always clearly understood. As a result of this misconception, Indians living in urban areas have often lost out on the opportunity to participate in other programs designed for disadvantaged groups. As a first step toward helping the urban Indians, I am instructing appropriate officials to do all they can to ensure that this misunderstanding is corrected.

But misunderstandings are not the most important problem confronting urban Indians. The biggest barrier faced by those Federal, State and local programs which are trying to serve urban Indians is the difficulty of locating and identifying them. Lost in the anonymity of the city, often cut off from family and friends, many urban Indians are slow to establish new community ties. Many drift from neighborhood to neighborhood; many shuttle back and forth between reservations and urban areas. Language and cultural differences compound these problems. As a result, Federal, State and local programs which are designed to help such persons often miss this most deprived and least understood segment of the urban poverty population.

This Administration is already taking steps which will help remedy this situation. In a joint effort, the Office of Economic Opportunity and the Department of Health, Education and Welfare will expand support to a total of seven urban Indian centers in major cities which will act as links between existing Federal, State and local service programs and the urban Indians. The Departments of Labor, Housing and Urban Development and Commerce have pledged to cooperate with such experimental urban centers and the Bureau of Indian Affairs has expressed its willingness to contract with these centers for the performance of relocation services which assist reservation Indians in their transition to urban employment.

These efforts represent an important beginning in recognizing and alleviating the severe problems faced by urban Indians. We hope to learn a great deal from these projects and to expand our efforts as rapidly as possible. I am directing the Office of Economic Opportunity to lead these efforts.

Richard Nixon
The White House
July 8, 1970

Senator Jackson Appoints Gerard
As Consultant on Indian Affairs

The Tribal Tribune (Colville Tribe), Feb. 8, 1971

Senator Henry M. Jackson, Chairman of the Senate Committee on Interior and Insular Affairs, today announced the appointment of Forrest J. Gerard to the professional staff of the Committee as a consultant on Indian affairs.

Gerard, an enrolled member of the Blackfeet Tribe of Montana, has served since November, 1967, as Director of the Office of Indian Affairs for the Department of Health, Education and Welfare.

Senator Jackson stated: "The staff responsibility for both the Indian Affairs and Territories and Insular Affairs Subcommittees has been held by one staff member, James H. Gamble, since the 87th Congress. In connection with the responsibilities of the Federal Government for the Trust Territory of the Pacific and other U.S. territories, an increasing amount of legislation has been before the Committee.

"These increased responsibilities are within the jurisdiction of the Subcommittee on Territories, in the future, will require Mr. Gamble's full time and attention.

"The Committee," Jackson said, "is fortunate in obtaining Mr. Gerard's services to assist in developing new policies and legislative measures designed to serve the needs and interests of the Nation's Indian people. He will, I believe, be in a unique position to work with the Committee in the development of innovative and responsive Federal programs."

Gerard's appointment, according to Jackson, sets the stage for the Interior Committee to launch a far-reaching review of the Indian programs during the 92nd Congress. The Senator added that the kind of intensive review he has in mind is vital at this time because of the "almost overwhelming social, economic and legal complexities which many Indian people encounter in seeking solutions to their problems."

"These complexities have evolved," Jackson said, "because of the unique historical legal relationship of Indian people with the Federal Government, as well as contemporary economic and social developments. Indian communities have traditionally looked to a single agency – the Bureau of Indian Affairs in the Department of the Interior – for protection of their lands and resources and assistance in solving the problems many face."

Indians, generally, qualify for these programs and services, not so much on the basis of their being Indian, but on the same basis as other Americans.

Jackson said that the Interior Committee's efforts in the 92nd Congress will not represent just another review of the so-called "Indian problem."

"We want our efforts to result in the establishment of a new Congressional Indian policy that will enable our first Americans to view the future with the assurance of constructive aid and services from the Federal Government, which will be responsive to the needs of Indian communities and Indian people."

Mr. Gerard was born in Browning, Montana, and was graduated from Montana State University with a B.A. in business administration in 1949.

News from: Senator Henry M. Jackson
For Immediate Release (Abridged)

Friday, February 1, 1974

Senator Henry M. Jackson today introduced a comprehensive Indian health care bill designed to expand and upgrade existing medical facilities and provide for additional medical personnel to staff Indian health delivery systems.

Jackson called his health package a natural and necessary companion to the Indian Financing Act passed earlier this Congress and the Indian Self-Determination and Educational Reform Act which his Interior and Insular Affairs Committee ordered reported to the Senate last Monday, January 28th.

Jackson said, "Each of these acts reaffirms a Congressional commitment to supply the economic and educational tools which the Indian people need to shape their own future. They will only be physically equal to this great task, however, if we take steps now to insure Indian Americans at least the minimum quality of care available to all other Americans."

Jackson noted that the Indian Health Service had made laudable progress despite severely limited resources. He added, "Yet diseases and health conditions that have posed little or no threat to most Americans for several generations are still commonplace for our Indian brothers."

Citing what he termed, "deplorable and heartbreaking health statistics for the Indian people," Jackson noted that incidences of tuberculosis, diabetes, gallbladder and respiratory ailments are far greater among Indians than the population at large; that the Indian infant mortality rate is almost one and one-half times the national average despite the fact that the Indian birth rate is about twice that for the general population; and the life expectancy for Indians is 64.9 years compared to 70.4 for other Americans.

Jackson said, "Another complication is the inordinately low ratio of doctors to patients in Indian communities – one doctor for every 1,080 Indians – compared to one physician for every 600 people on a national scale. Fewer doctors and related medical professionals are entering the Indian health field every year, and the end of the so-called, "Doctor-Draft," spells a further depletion of medical staffing.

The legislation proposes:
- Scholarship grants to medical and related health-field students who agree to serve the Indian Community upon completing professional training, and to Indian high school graduates who demonstrate an aptitude for pre-medical, pre-dental or pre-osteopathy training.
- Special allowances which enable physicians recruited to staff Indian medical services to leave their duty stations for prescribed time periods to benefit from professional consultation and refresher training courses.
- Sufficient appropriations over a five year period to supply the additional health personnel needed to reduce or eliminate the tremendous backlog of Indian patients awaiting medical attention.
- Allocations of $400 million over a five year period to supply the additional $470 million for vitally needed safe water and sanitary waste disposal facilities in both existing and new Indian homes and communities.
- Direct Medicare and Medicaid payments to Indian health hospitals instead of to the general Treasury in order to give

Indians greater access to benefits from social welfare programs currently available to all Americans.

- An evaluation system that requires the Secretary of HEW to submit a detailed review and assessment of the above programs including recommendations for additional programs and assistance to insure that Indians enjoy a health status equal to all Americans.

President Gerald R. Ford: Statement on Signing the Indian Health Care Improvement Act

October 1, 1976

I am signing S. 522, the Indian Health Care Improvement Act.

This bill is not without its faults, but after personal review I have decided that the well-documented needs for improvement in Indian health manpower, services, and facilities outweigh the defects in the bill.

While spending for Indian Health Service activities has grown from $128 million in FY 1970 to $425 million in FY 1977, Indian people still lag behind the American people as a whole in achieving and maintaining good health. I am signing this bill because of my own conviction that our first Americans should not be last in opportunity.

Some of the authorizations in this bill are duplicative of existing authorities, and there is an unfortunate proliferation of narrow categorical programs. Nevertheless, S. 522 is a statement of direction of effort which is commendable.

Title VII of this bill provides for future reports to the Congress from the Secretary of Health, Education, and Welfare, including a review of progress under the terms of the new act. I believe the administration can in this way bring to the attention of the Congress any changes needed to improve the provisions of S. 522.

On balance, this bill is a positive step, and I am pleased to sign it.

ABOUT THE AUTHOR

Mark Trahant is a writer, teacher and a "Twitter poet." He has been writing about Indian Country for more than three decades. Mark spent much of 2009 and 2010 writing about health care reform as a Kaiser Media Fellow.

He has taught about social media and its impact on democracy at the University of Idaho and the University of Colorado at Boulder. The course explored the idea of how a nation can tell its story in 140 characters and the relationship between social media and the news media. Twitter & Democracy began with a history of the media and disruptive change, and then explored how the values of professional media are being rewritten, ignored or transmitted through social media, including MySpace, Facebook and Twitter. For several years, Trahant has been writing daily "news poems" on Twitter. These four-line rhymes are based on current events under the handle "NewsRimes4lines."

He is also the former editor of the editorial page for the Seattle Post-Intelligencer where he chaired the daily editorial board, directed a staff of writers, editors and a cartoonist. Trahant has been chairman and chief executive officer at the Robert C. Maynard Institute for Journalism Education. The Oakland, Calif.-based non-profit is the country's premier institute for providing advanced training and services nationally to help news media reflect diversity in content, staffing and business operations. He also has been a columnist at The Seattle Times; publisher of the Moscow-Pullman Daily News in Moscow, Idaho; executive news editor of The Salt Lake Tribune; a reporter at the Arizona Republic in Phoenix; and has worked at several tribal newspapers, including his tribal newspaper, The Sho-Ban News.

Trahant was a juror for the Pulitzer Prize in 2004 and 2005.

He is a member of Idaho's Shoshone-Bannock Tribes. He is married to LeNora Begay Trahant and they have two boys, Marvin and Elias. They live in Fort Hall, Idaho.

Follow Mark on Twitter. He can be found @TrahantReports or his poetry @newsrimes4lines. You can also follow @lastgreatbattle on Twitter and join "The Last Great Battle" fan page on Facebook.